115 CLASSIC AMERICAN PATCHWORK QUILT PATTERNS

Liberty Star (95), pp. 171, 172

Maggie Malone

Sterling Publishing Co., Inc.   New York
Distributed in the U.K. by Blandford Press

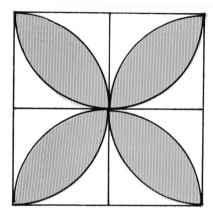

Lafayette Orange Peel (64), pp. 119, 120

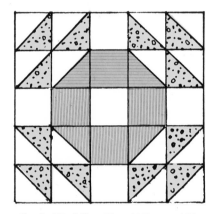

Single Wedding Ring (90), pp. 162

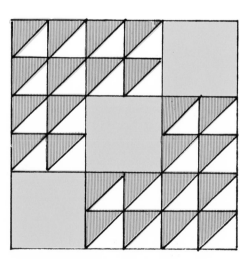

Cut Glass Dish (20), pp. 53, 54

Library of Congress Cataloging in Publication Data

Malone, Maggie, 1942–
    115 classic American patchwork quilt patterns.

    Rev. ed. of: Classic American patchwork quilt patterns. 1977.
    Includes indexes.
    1. Quilting—United States—Patterns. 2. Patchwork—United States—Patterns. I. Malone, Maggie, 1942–
Classic American patchwork quilt patterns. II. Title
III. Title: One hundred fifteen classic American patchwork quilt patterns.
TT835.M345   1984   746.9′7041   83-18180
ISBN 0-8069-5512-0
ISBN 0-8069-7846-5 (pbk.)

Color section designed by Barbara Busch

Revised edition © 1984 by Maggie Malone
First edition © 1977 by Maggie Malone under
the title "Classic American Patchwork
Quilt Patterns."

Published in 1984 by Sterling Publishing Co., Inc.
Two Park Avenue, New York, N.Y. 10016
Distributed in Australia by Oak Tree Press Co., Ltd.
P.O. Box K514 Haymarket, Sydney 2000, N.S.W.
Distributed in the United Kingdom by Blandford Press
Link House, West Street, Poole, Dorset BH15 1LL, England
Distributed in Canada by Oak Tree Press Ltd.
℅ Canadian Manda Group, P.O. Box 920, Station U
Toronto, Ontario, Canada M8Z 5P9
Manufactured in the United States of America

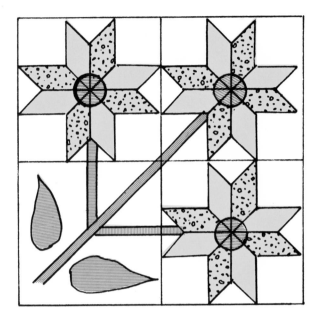

Triple Sunflower (108), pp. 193, 194

CONTENTS

The Color Index has been color-coordinated. The reader who has a pretty piece of yellow calico, for example, which he or she wants to use can turn to the pages showing suggestions for yellow and perhaps find the ideal design. The number within the parentheses in each caption of the Color Index refers to the number of the pattern; the page numbers which follow are the pages in which the pattern is to be found.

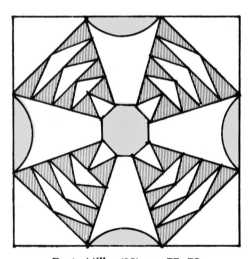

Dusty Miller (38), pp. 77, 78

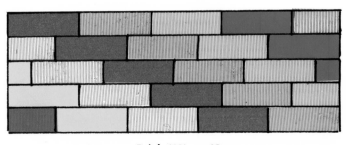

Brick (12), p. 42

Friendship Knot (42), pp. 85–87

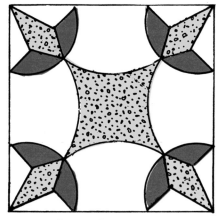

Turkey Tracks (110), p. 196

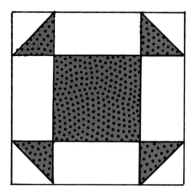

Puss in the Corner (82), pp. 147, 148

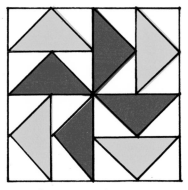

Dutchman's Puzzle (37), p. 76

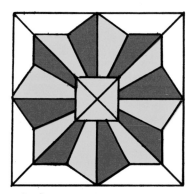

Sunbeam (104), pp. 185, 186

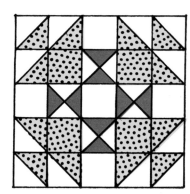

Handy Andy (52), p. 99

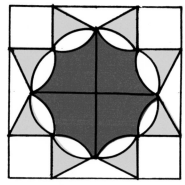

French Star (97), p. 176

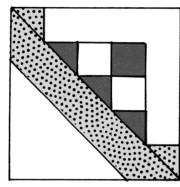

King's Crown (60), pp. 111, 112

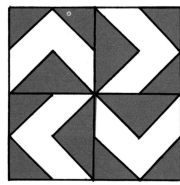

Swastika (107), p. 192

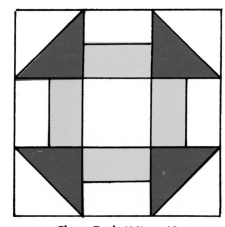

Churn Dash (16), p. 48

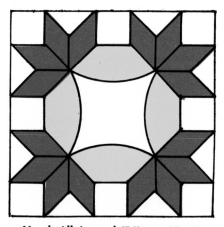

Hands All Around (51), pp. 97, 98

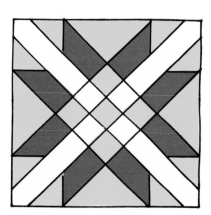

Mexican Cross (66), p. 123

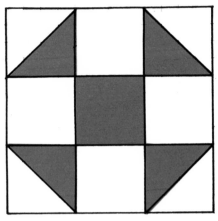

Shoofly II (89), p. 161

Aunt Sukey's Choice (2), pp. 26, 27

Barbara Frietchie Rose (43), p. 88

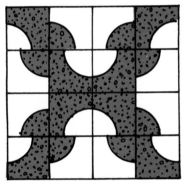

No Name (34), p. 71

Drunkard's Trail (36), pp. 73–75

Odd Fellows' Chain (73), pp. 133, 134

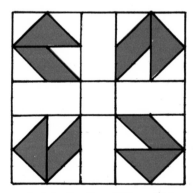

Jack in the Box (56), p. 104

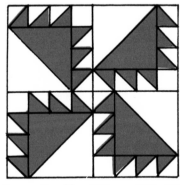

Kansas Troubles (59), pp. 109, 110

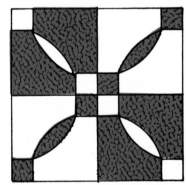

Rose Dream (86), pp. 156, 157

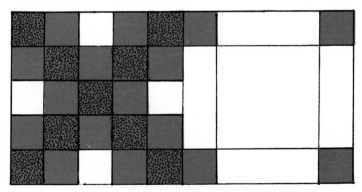

Double Irish Chain (23), pp. 60, 61

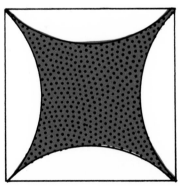

Robbing Peter to Pay Paul I (84), pp. 151, 152

Indian Puzzle (54), pp. 101, 102

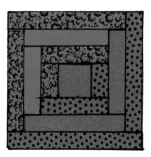

Log Cabin (61), pp. 114–116

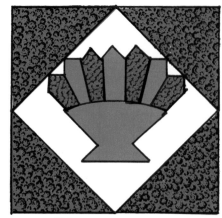

Dobbin's Fan (39), pp. 79–81

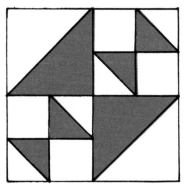

Crosses & Losses (77), p. 139

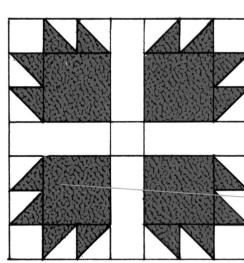
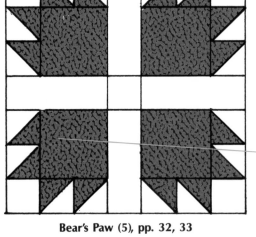

Bear's Paw (5), pp. 32, 33

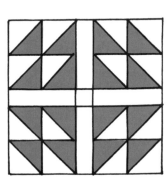

Flying Geese (46), p. 93

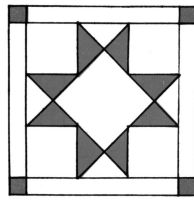

Aunt Eliza's Star (92), pp. 165, 166

Box (11), pp. 40, 41

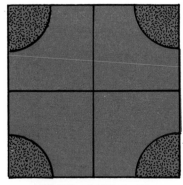

Mill Wheel (33), p. 71

Sugar Loaf (103), pp. 183, 184

Necktie, (70), p. 128

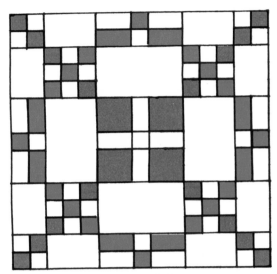

Burgoyne Surrounded (13), p. 43

Queen's Pride (83), pp. 149, 150

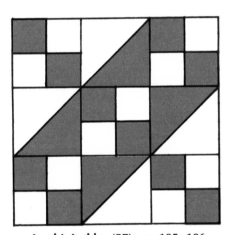

Jacob's Ladder (57), pp. 105, 106

Birds in the Air II (9), p. 37

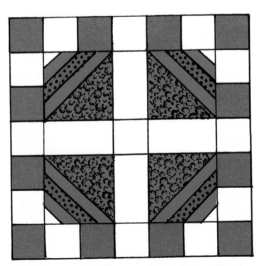

Lincoln's Platform (65), pp. 121, 122

Dove in the Window (26), pp. 64, 65

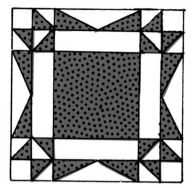

Robbing Peter to Pay Paul II (85),
pp. 153, 154

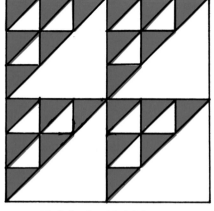

Birds in the Air I (8), p. 36

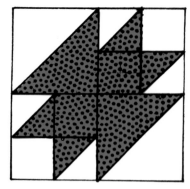

Anvil (76), p. 139

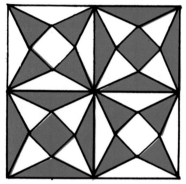

World Without End (115),
pp. 203, 204

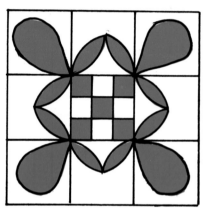

Blue Blazes (10), pp. 38, 39

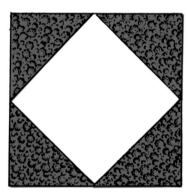

Shoofly I (88), pp. 159, 160

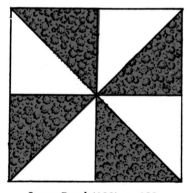

Sugar Bowl (102), p. 182

Lady of the Lake (63), p. 117, 118

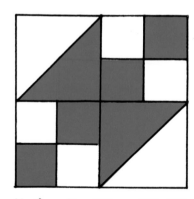

Northern Star (96), pp. 173–175

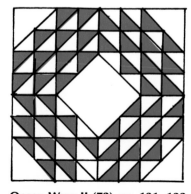

Ocean Wave II (72), pp. 131, 132

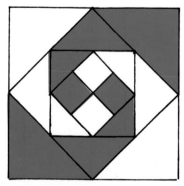

Monkey Wrench (68), pp. 125, 126

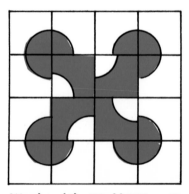

Wonder of the World (29), p. 69

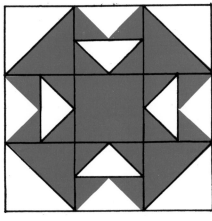

Double T (24), p. 62

Delectable Mountains (22) pp. 57–59

Garden Path (44), pp. 89, 90

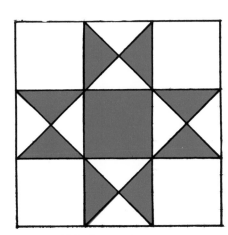

Ohio Star (99), p. 179

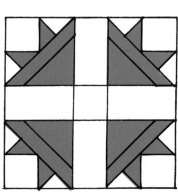

Cross & Crown (18), pp. 50, 51

Hourglass (53), p. 100

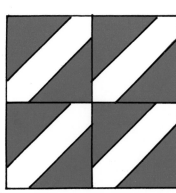

Indian Hatchet (55), p. 103

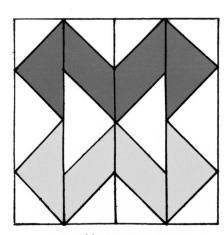

Double Z (25), p. 63

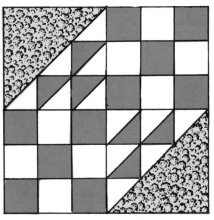

Batle of the Alamo (1), p. 25

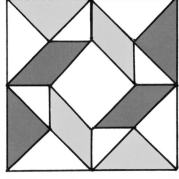

Windblown Square (113), p. 200

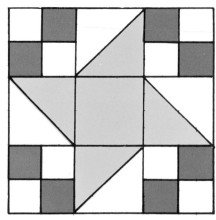

Milky Way (67), p. 124

Wild Goose Chase I (111),
p. 197, 198

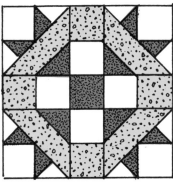

David & Goliath (21), pp. 55, 56

Joseph's Coat (58), pp. 107, 108

Drunkard's Path (28), p. 68

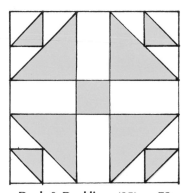

Duck & Ducklings (35), p. 72

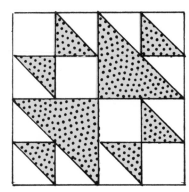

Old Maid's Puzzle (75),
pp. 137, 138

Arkansas Traveler (6) pp. 34, 35

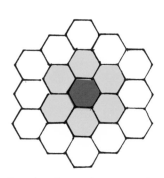

Grandmother's Flower Garden
(48), p. 95

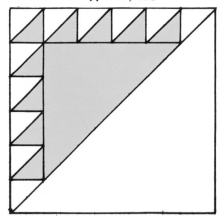

Sawtooth (87), pp. 157, 158

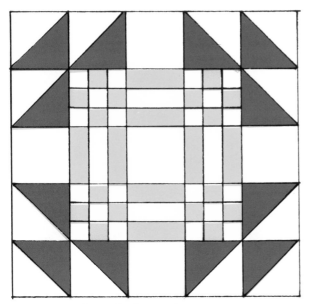

Goose in the Pond (47), p. 94

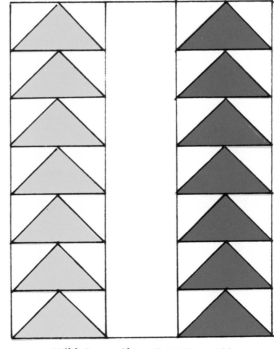

Wild Goose Chase II (112), p. 199

North Carolina Lily (71), pp. 129, 130

Corn & Beams (17), p. 49

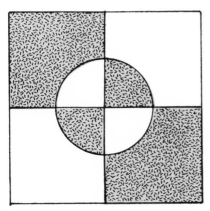

Vine of Friendship (32), p. 70

Stonemason's Puzzle (100), p. 180

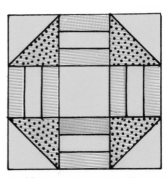

Golden Gate (45), pp. 91, 92

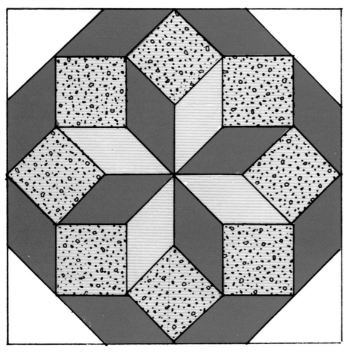

Rolling Star (98), pp. 177, 178

Prickly Pear (81), pp. 145, 146

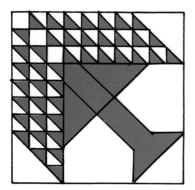

Pine Tree (80), pp. 143, 144

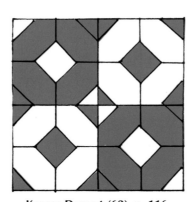

Kansas Dugout (62), p. 116

Fool's Puzzle (30), p. 69

Our Village Green (74), pp. 135, 136

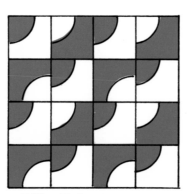

Falling Timbers (31), p. 70

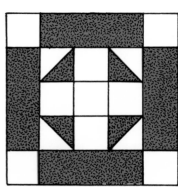

Philadelphia Pavement (79), pp. 141, 142

Cactus Flower (14), pp. 44, 45

Wood Lily (114), pp. 201, 202

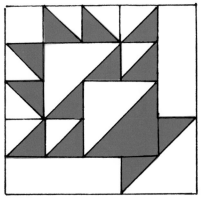

Grape Basket (4), pp. 30, 31

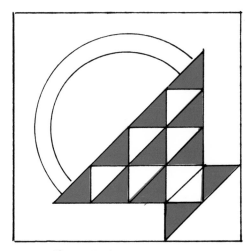

Flower Basket (3), pp. 28, 29

Prairie Queen (78), p. 140

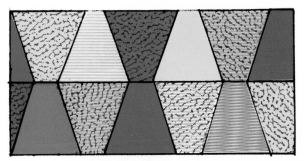

Tumbler (109), p. 195

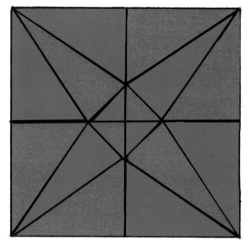

Crossed Canoes (19), p. 52

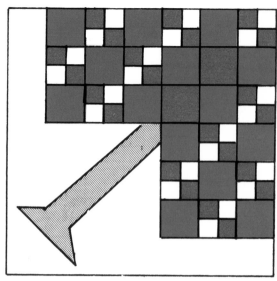

Tree of Temptation (106), pp. 189–191

Streak of Lightning (101), p. 181

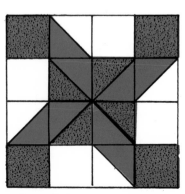

Clay's Choice (15), pp. 46, 47

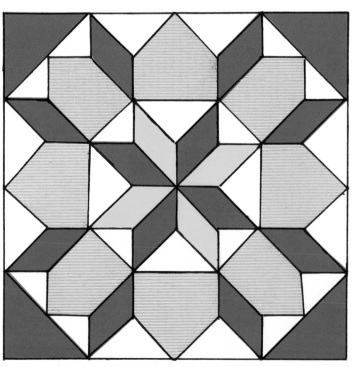

Star of Bethlehem (93), pp. 167, 168

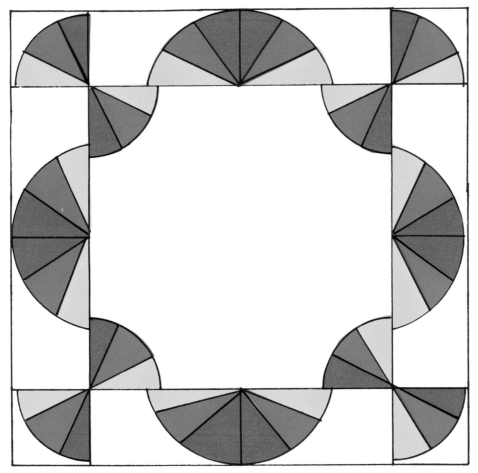

Mohawk Trail (69), p. 127

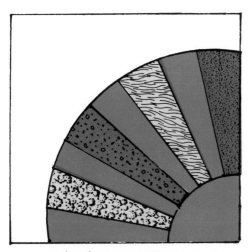

Grandmother's Fan (41) pp. 83, 84

Fancy Dresden Plate (27), pp. 66, 67

Sunflower (105), pp. 187, 188

Beggar Block (7), pp. 34, 35

Milady's Fan (40), p. 82

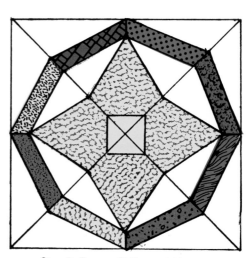

Star & Crown (94), pp. 169, 170

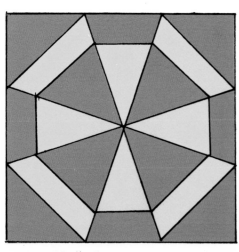

Spider Web (91), pp. 163, 164

Ocean Wave (49), p. 96

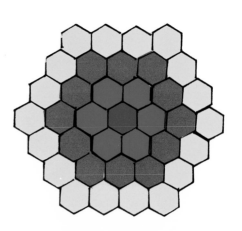

Honeycomb (50), p. 96

INTRODUCTION

Quilting arrived in America with the first European settlers, but through the thrift and ingenuity of the pioneer woman, patchwork quilting as we know it today evolved into a uniquely American art form.

The quilt patterns developed by these women reflected the day-to-day lives of their creators. The garden, the barnyard, the sky, the sea—all the beauty and grandeur of this new land was translated into their quilts. Their battles, their heroes, the glory and sorrow of American history, can be found in the quilt patterns they devised. Thus we owe a debt of gratitude to the generations of American women who, in spite of technological advances, took pride in keeping this craft alive and carefully preserving this rich heritage for us.

My interest in quilting began in the sixties. It was a completely new field to me, one about which I knew absolutely nothing. At that time, it was difficult to find any information on the subject. The public library had few books on quilting and only occasionally would a magazine even mention the subject. Within the past twelve years, however, there has been a great resurgence of interest in patchwork quilting. Books and magazine articles on the subject have proliferated. Still, to reproduce an authentic quilt, I found myself going from book to book to gather the necessary information. Even then many articles provided only a scale drawing of the patterns. I didn't want to draft a pattern, I wanted to make a quilt. And it would have been much easier if the author had told me how much fabric I needed to buy. Some articles didn't even mention block size so that I could estimate the yardage myself without first making up the block. Unless stated otherwise, yardages are for a forty-five inch fabric.

I also found myself interested in the history of the patterns and how they were traditionally assembled. That took a lot of hunting. So often, a pattern would appear with no color recommendations or instructions as to how the top should be set together. When our grandmothers made the quilt, did they set it solid, alternately pieced with plain blocks, or use lattice strips between blocks? A lot of my information was garnered from decorating magazines which occasionally would show an antique quilt in a room setting and give a brief description of the quilt and its age.

From these sources I gradually began to compile my own collection of patterns, including all the information I wanted to know about a quilt pattern. Every pattern given in this book includes a picture of the block, full-size patterns, yardage requirements for the quilt size given, and traditional colors where possible. The block size has also been given in case you wish to change the size of the quilt. Suggestions are also given for setting the quilt top together.

Each pattern is at least fifty years old and, where possible, I have tried to give the earliest known date of its appearance. Along with the date, any background information available, such as history or legends surrounding it, has been included.

As the pioneer woman entered new territories, her quilt patterns went with her. It became common practice to change the name of the older pattern to better reflect her new surroundings. Hence, many old patterns have been known by different names at different times and in different parts of the country; and in some instances the same name was given to completely different patterns. The pattern *Swastika*, for example, has had at least eight different names. To help sort out these differences, each pattern has been cross-referenced in the text to show the variant names by which it has been known, and the index lists the names of every quilt mentioned.

Some of the patterns include specific quilting directions; for those that do not, it is a general rule to quilt one-eighth inch from all seams. If there are large areas or the pattern has especially large pieces making up a block, a filling stitch at half-inch intervals should be used. For those patterns set with alternate plain blocks or with lattice strips, use a large floral or feather motif to fill in the block. The lattice strips can be quilted in a cable or vine pattern.

Those patterns that do not include specific sewing instructions can be easily assembled by following the block diagram, which has been carefully drawn to show where all the pieces should go.

In making your own quilt, I recommend that you use only new, good-quality fabrics, for the finished quilt will then last much longer and be better able to withstand the hard usage expected of it. If you want to make a quilt from your children's worn-out clothing or other used fabric, make it a special quilt and don't expect too much use from it. Worn fabrics have already seen their best days. You are devoting a lot of time and effort to make your quilt beautiful; I'm sure you will want it around for many years.

Along the same lines, for an everyday quilt, I see nothing wrong in using the sewing machine for all the straight seams. Even the straight-line quilting can be done on the machine, though I do not recommend this procedure for a very special quilt or for one that you intend to enter for judging, since such special quilts are judged for workmanship as well as design.

This book is the result of years of interest and research in patchwork quilting. I hope you will find it a valuable and much used addition to your needlework library.

Maggie Malone

SOME GENERAL INSTRUCTIONS

SELECTING FABRICS:

Just about every type of fabric imaginable has been used for quiltmaking. In the 1700s, the highly prized Indian chintzes were the favorite fabric of quiltmakers. However, these fabrics were expensive, and, therefore, used only for "best" quilts. Every little scrap was utilized in some way. Utility tops were often made from wool with linsey-woolsey backings. As a testament to the durability of wool, many examples have survived to the present and can be seen in museums around the country.

Velvets, velveteens, silks and satins have been used at different times, but the fragility of these fabrics limits their use to special quilts that will not see hard wear.

Many home sewers have used up their scrap double-knit fabrics by incorporating them into a quilt. The double knits have a hard finish that is difficult to push a needle through so use of the sewing machine for quilting should be considered, if these fabrics are to be used.

The favored fabric for quiltmaking, however, is 100% cotton. Its smooth, soft finish allows the needle to glide through the quilt easily during both the piecing and quilting processes. But cotton is not always easy to come by and even when it is available, your choice may be limited as to colors and prints. My personal preference is for the cotton/polyester blends. They are always available, come in a wide range of colors and prints, and work up beautifully. Over the years, my experience has been that they wear well, don't shrink and don't fade. And in spite of all the horror stories and advice to the contrary, I never preshrink fabric. On this point, I would not think of advising you not to preshrink; I am just stating that I never have. I may be sorry some day, but so far so good.

Quilting is known primarily as a scrap craft and worn-out clothing has often been used for this purpose. In recent years, even blue jeans and T-shirts have been used for making special memory quilts for children. When using worn clothing, however, be sure to use only those portions that are not worn. You're going to put a lot of work into your quilt and any borderline pieces of cloth will wear out before the rest of the quilt.

Buying fabric for a quilt can get expensive, so when you come across sales be sure to buy as much fabric as you can. Discount stores generally have lower prices than your local fabric shop. Check around for remnant stores. These stores sell first-quality goods that have been discontinued by the manufacturer or overstocked. In those areas near manufacturers, you can find outlet stores that have fantastic prices on fabric. One of my favorite sources for fabric is sheets. They are periodically on sale at considerable savings and the white and pastel colors are great for background fabric.

TEMPLATES

Your template is your most important tool in making a quilt. It must be accurate to ensure that the fabric pieces go together properly. My first step is always to make a full-size drawing of the block, using the pattern pieces given, to be sure that they are correct. This is quicker than making a sample block. I can make any corrections necessary on the drawing before making my templates.

Templates can be made from heavy cardboard backed with sandpaper to prevent slippage or from plastic that is backed with sandpaper. The plastic is a better material since it doesn't wear down with use.

To make a template, trace the pattern piece onto white typing paper. Glue the paper to your template material and cut it out. When adding the seam allowance, you have two choices. Once you have drawn the pattern onto the white paper, you can add the seam allowance before you cut out the template. The template will then include the seam allowance, and when cutting, you just cut on the line drawn. The second method is to make your template the exact size of the finished pattern piece. Trace around it on the fabric, spacing the patterns far enough apart to allow for a seam allowance when cutting. Your cut piece will show the seamline, giving you a guide for sewing.

PIECING THE QUILT

Your second most important tool in making a quilt is your iron. When each seam is finished, press it before joining to another seam. The seam allowance is usually pressed to one side. When joining two seams together, press one seam to the left and the other seam to the right. The two pieces will slide right into the seamline making a perfect match.

I do all piecing on the sewing machine. As an example, for "Battle of the Alamo," I will run all the C-units through the machine in a long strip, then take the strip to the ironing board to press and cut apart. Since I do use the sewing machine, I generally press the seams open rather than to one side.

SETTING THE TOP

The final step in assembling the quilt top is the setting. The simplest method is to alternate plain and pieced blocks. With this setting you only have to piece half as many blocks and you have more space for decorative quilting.

Many designs require that the blocks be set solid to bring out the pattern. Often, a secondary pattern emerges to give added interest to the overall design.

The use of lattice strips to separate the blocks is another popular setting method, especially if the pattern has been executed in scrap fabrics. The lattice strips pull the design together into a coherent whole. And again, you don't need to piece as many blocks because the lattice strips add to the size of the quilt with little additional work.

Many blocks are designed to be set on the diagonal, but you should also try some of your favorite patterns set diagonally. The change of perspective will give you an entirely different quilt.

Lattice strips are also effective on a diagonally set quilt. They can either blend in by being the same color as the background blocks or you can set the design off by using color in the strips. The long lines of solid color enhance and accentuate a diagonal design.

QUILTING

Quilting is the finishing touch to your patchwork top. The primary purpose of the quilting stitches is to hold the three layers of the quilt together, but it has evolved into a highly decorative design element.

A quilt is a sandwich of three layers: the pieced top, the filler, and the backing.

Fillers or Batts

Cotton batts. This is a cotton material in batt form. It must be closely quilted, with no more than an inch between the quilting lines because the batt will shift and bunch up when washed. It gives a rather flat appearance to the finished quilting.

Bonded polyester batts. This is a polyester material which has been treated to hold the fibres together. It is easy to work with since the layers of the batt will not shred or tear, giving a smooth, uniform surface. The finished quilt has a higher loft and the quilting stitches stand out in relief. It need not be quilted as closely as cotton batts; two to four inches is usually sufficient.

Unbonded batts. These batts give a very soft, fluffy appearance to the finished quilt. Like the bonded batts, they are easy to work with during the sewing step, but care must be taken when spreading the batt on the top or it will shred, leaving thick and thin spots. You will have to pull off pieces from the thick spots or along the edges to fill in the thin spots. It, too, can be quilted two to four inches apart.

Lining or Backing Fabrics

Your choice is varied as to what you use to back your quilt; yard goods seamed to the width required, flannel, sheets or lightweight blankets are all suitable. You might even try a reversible quilt, piecing both the top and the backing.

Marking the Quilt Top

For many patterns, quilting along each side of the seamline will bring out the pattern to best advantage. In this case, no marking is necessary. For straight lines, you can use dressmaker's carbon and a tracing wheel, or even a carpenter's chalk line. For the chalk line, have someone hold one end of the line, and pull it across the top. Hold your end down tightly and shape the line. The nice thing about both of these methods is that they wash out easily. In fact, the chalk may disappear too easily, flaking off before the quilting is completed.

For more intricate designs, use a template and a soft lead pencil. Better yet, try a dressmaker's pencil. It always washes out.

Assembling the Quilt

Lay the top wrong-side-up on a large, flat surface. I've found the floor to be the most convenient place. Spread the batting over the top and smooth it out.

Seam the backing fabric together to the width of the quilt top, plus one inch or two inches all around. This extra allowance is especially important when doing machine quilting. The extra margin allows for any shifting of the fabric as you sew.

Hand quilting. Baste the three layers together diagonally from corner to corner, then three or four rows up and down the quilt and crosswise. The quilt is now ready to be placed in the frame.

The quilting stitch is a small running stitch, 10 to 15 stitches to the inch. Pull the thread through so that the end is in the batting. Take a small backstitch, bringing the needle to the top. Push the needle through to the back, bring it up a short distance away, and repeat, following your quilting lines.

Machine quilting. First, do not baste the layers of the quilt together. My experience has been that the fabric tends to pile up on the basting stitches, causing puckers and ripples. By cutting the fabric slightly larger for the back, I can smooth the top in front of the presser foot, taking out any wrinkles as I sew.

Second, loosen the pressure on the presser foot. This helps cut down on shifting and pushing of the fabric, which is the major problem in machine quilting.

A large table on which to sew is an absolute must. It helps keep the quilt flat, cutting down on the amount of shifting you will experience. Position your machine at one end of the table so you can spread the quilt out.

Slide the edge of the quilt under the presser foot and roll it up to the center. The center section is the most difficult because so much fabric is rolled under the machine. As you move out towards the edges, it gets easier. Following the quilting line from the center, stitch to the outer edge of the quilt, smoothing the fabric as you go. Do two or three rows in this direction, then turn the quilt and go in the opposite direction. This alternating technique helps keep the quilt smooth and flat.

If your top is of a simple design that requires only straight-line stitching, you can start at one end of the quilt and work to the other end. In this case, the backing fabric should be longer on the end towards which you are sewing so that any shift in the fabric is covered by the backing when finished. Always start sewing at the same end.

By the Block

This is an easy way to quilt, either by hand or machine, because you are working with only one block at a time. For intricate designs, this method is by far the best, since the block is easy to manipulate under the needle.

Cut the filler the size of the finished block, and if using the sewing machine, cut the backing one inch larger than the block. Otherwise, cut it the same size. Lay the three layers together and quilt in the design, being sure that you do not quilt beyond the seamline into the seam allowance.

To assemble the blocks. Turn back the seam allowance of the backing and push the filler out of the way. Lay the quilted blocks with the right sides together and stitch the seams, being sure not to catch in the backing or the filler. Continue adding blocks until the first row is complete, then repeat for each succeeding row. Join the rows in the same manner.

Finishing the back. Smooth the batting down and trim off any excess. It should meet in the middle of the seam. Smooth one side of the backing down. Turn under the seam allowance on the other seam and lay over the first one. Stitch with a slipstitch.

   A really nice finish for the back is to place lattice strips over the seams and stitch in place.

EASY

Quilt Size:		60" x 72"
Block Size:		12"
Blocks in Quilt:		30
		(5 across by 6 down)

Material:
2 yds. Gold flowered
3 yds. White
3 yds. Blue

Pieces per Block			per Quilt
A	2	Gold	60
B	10	Blue	300
	8	White	240
C	12	White	360
	6	Blue	180

in color p. 10

1. Battle of the Alamo

Sewing Instructions: Break the block into four squares, two assembled from Piece B, and two assembled from Pieces A and C. After completing the four units, assemble them to form the whole block. Finished blocks are set side by side.

Border: Add a narrow border, or just bind off.

Quilting: Quilt 1/8" from all seams. The diagonal corner block may be filled with straight stitching 1/2" apart or with a small floral motif.

ADD 1/4" SEAM ALLOWANCE

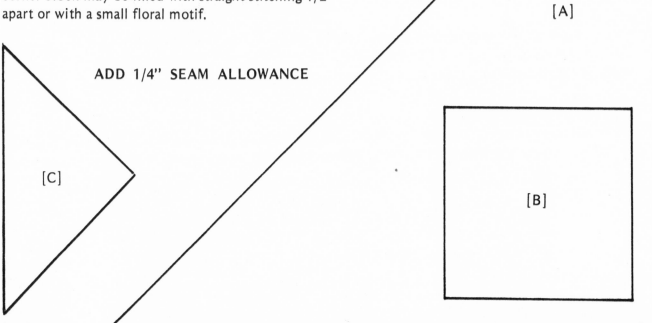

EASY

Quilt Size:	72" x 84"	
Block Size:	12"	
Blocks in Quilt:	42	
	(6 across by 7 down)	

Material:
  5 yds. White
  2-3/4 yds. Color
  2/3 yds. Print

Pieces	per Block		per Quilt
A	1	Print	42
B	12	White	504
	4	Color	168
C	8	Color	336
D	4	White	168
E	8	White	336

in color p. 5

2. Aunt Sukey's Choice

By making all the colored pieces the same and setting the quilt diagonally, this pattern becomes *Puss in the Corner.*

   Sewing Instructions: Cut out design units adding 1/4" seam allowance. Break this block into eight smaller blocks; assemble each of these, and then join around the center square.

   This is an allover design, so the blocks are set together side by side. The edges can be simply bound off, or you can add a narrow border.

   Quilting: Quilt 1/8" from all seams.

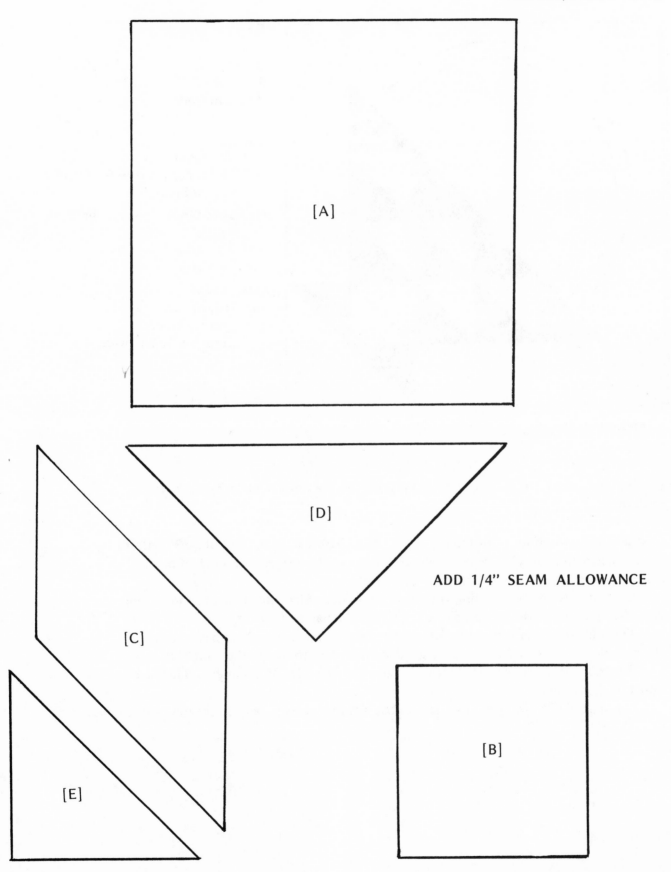

[A]

[D]

[C]

ADD 1/4" SEAM ALLOWANCE

[E]

[B]

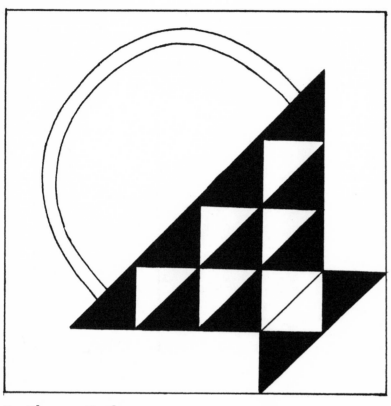

EASY

Quilt Size:	92" x 103"
Block Size:	12"
Blocks in Quilt:	32

(20 pieced, 12 plain; 4 across by 5 down)

Material:
- 9 yds. White
- 3 yds. Color (usually Blue, Green, or Brown)

Pieces per Block			per Quilt
A	11	Color	220
	7	White	140
B	1	Color	32

Other Units:
- 14 Half Blocks
- 4 Quarter Blocks
  Border, 9" - 12" wide

in color p. 13

3. Flower Basket

This pattern dates from at least 1830 and is probably the most popular basket pattern of all time.

Sewing Instructions: Cut thirty-two 13" blocks for background. Cut a 12" pattern in half diagonally, add 1/4" seam allowance, and cut out fourteen of these half blocks. Following the same procedure, cut four quarter blocks.

Cut out pattern units, adding 1/4" seam allowance. Piece the basket as shown, and then applique to the background block. Applique the handle in place.

The quilt top is set diagonally with a plain block alternating with a pieced one. The half blocks and quarter blocks are set along the edges to square the quilt.

Border: A plain white strip 9" to 12" wide can be added as a border and quilted with a feather pattern.

Quilting: Quilt 1/8" from each seam. Use a feather-wreath pattern for the plain blocks.

ADD 1/4" SEAM ALLOWANCE

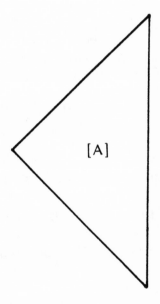

[A]

[B]

4. Grape Basket

EASY

					per Quilt
Quilt Size:			68" x 82"		
Block Size:			10"		
Blocks in Quilt:			32		

(20 pieced, 12 plain; 4 across by 5 down)

Material:
  6 yds. White
  2-1/2 yds. Color

Pieces per Block				per Quilt
A	1	White		20
B	12	Color		260
	4	White		80
C	2	White		40
D	3	White		60
	1	Color		20
E	2	White		40

Other Units:
12 Plain Blocks, 11" square
14 Half Blocks
 4 Quarter Blocks
    Border, 6" wide

in color p. 13

Sewing Instructions: Cut out design units adding 1/4" seam allowance. You will need 12 plain blocks cut 11" square, 14 half squares (be sure to add seam allowance to diagonal edge), and four quarter squares.

Follow the drawing to assemble the basket. The base of the basket consists of one color D and two color B.

The blocks are set diagonally, with alternate rows of plain blocks. The half and quarter squares fill out the edges.

Border: Add a 6" border. To make a large quilt, use a wide border.

Quilting: Quilt 1/8" from all seams. On the border quilt a flowing feather or vine motif.

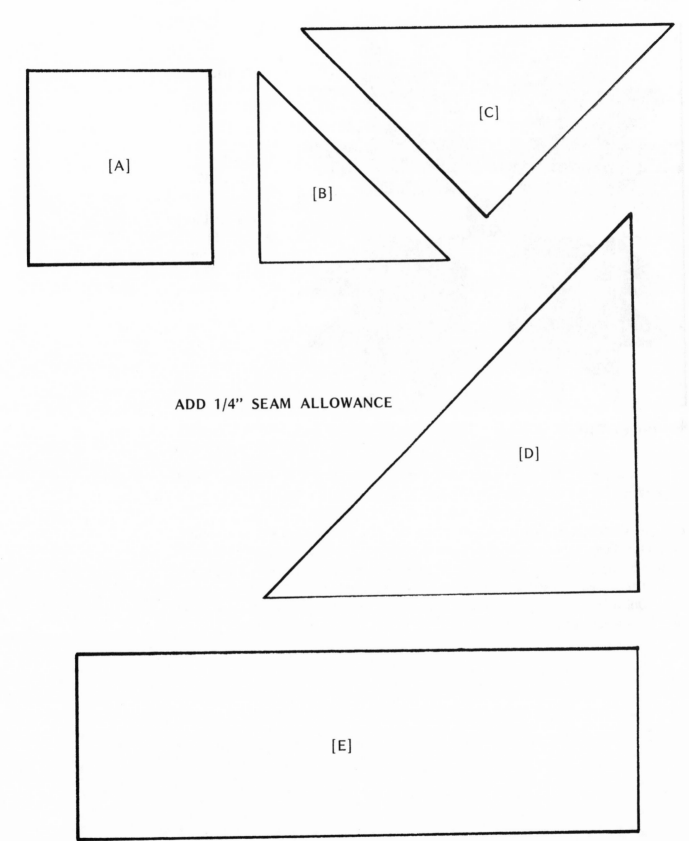

[A]

[B]

[C]

[D]

ADD 1/4" SEAM ALLOWANCE

[E]

EASY

Quilt Size:		72" x 79"
Block Size:		12"
Blocks in Quilt:		36

(18 pieced, 18 plain; 6 across by 6 down)

Material:
5 yds. White
3 yds. Color Print

Pieces per Block			per Quilt
A	1	Print	18
	4	White	72
B	16	White	288
	16	Print	288
C	2	White	72
D	4	Print	72

in color p. 6

5. Bear's Paw

This is another of those popular patterns having many names. It was called *Hand of Friendship* by the Quakers, *Bear Tracks* in Ohio, and *Duck's Foot in the Mud* in New York.

Sewing Instructions: Break the block into four smaller blocks and assemble them. Then sew Piece C between two of these smaller blocks. Sew a long strip made of C-A-C; add this strip to the previously assembled pieces. Repeat to complete the block.

The pieced blocks are set alternately with plain blocks.

Quilting: On the pieced blocks, quilt 1/8" from all seams. A small motif might be used on each of the D squares.

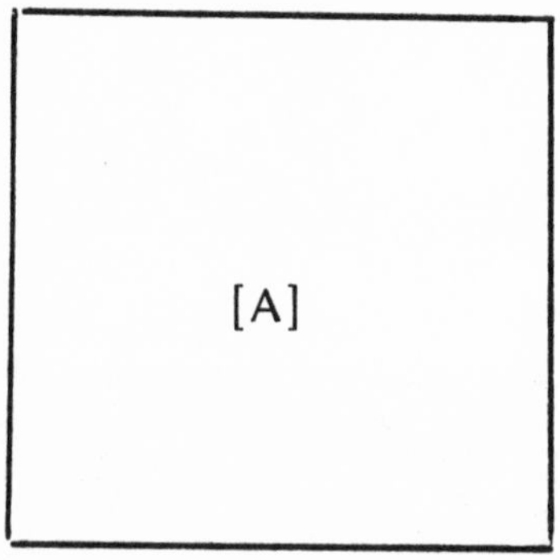

[A]

ADD 1/4" SEAM ALLOWANCE

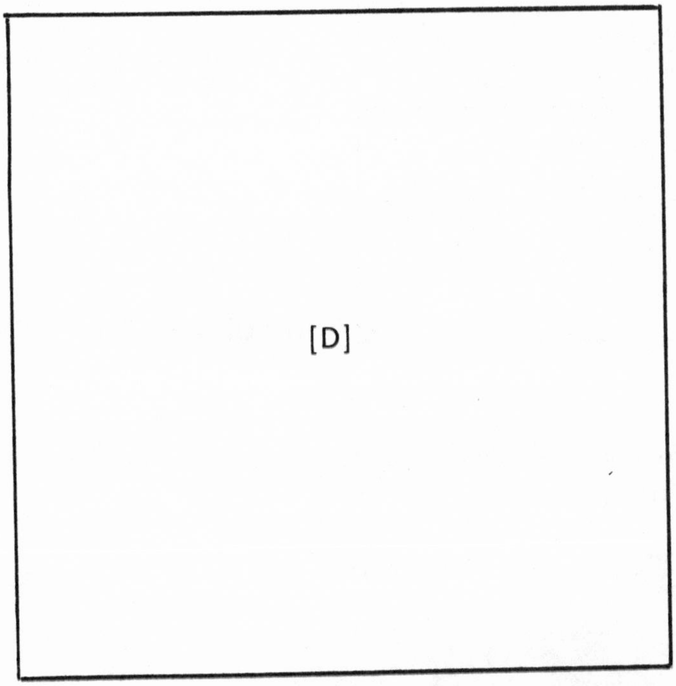

[D]

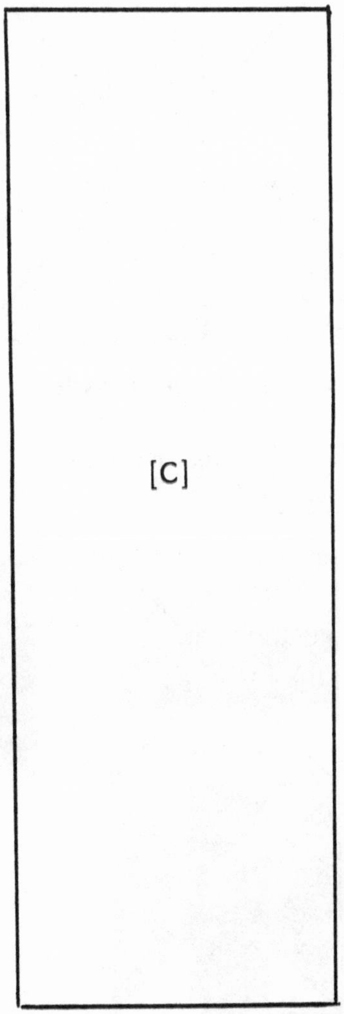

[C]

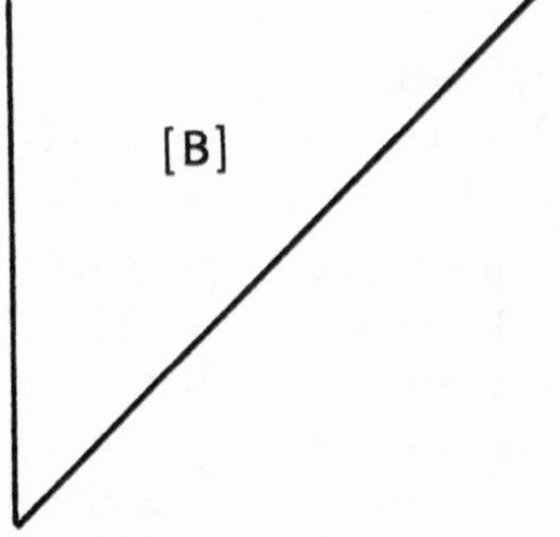

[B]

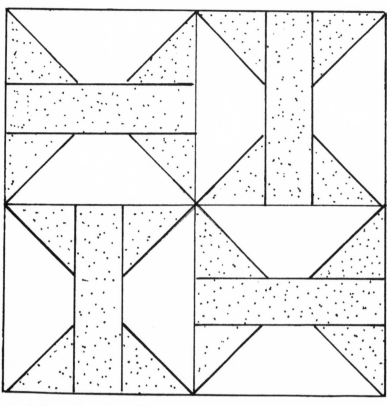

EASY

Quilt Size:	80" x 90"	
Block Size:	10"	
Blocks in Quilt:	72	
Material:	(8 across by 9 down)	

5-2/3 yds. Print
3-1/2 yds. Light Color

Pieces per Block			per Quilt
B	8	Light Color	576
C	16	Print	1152
D	4	Print	288

Sewing Instructions: Blocks are set side by side, eight rows across and nine rows down.

in color p. 10

6. Arkansas Traveler

Sewing Instructions: These two blocks use identical pattern pieces. Just follow the diagrams to make two completely different quilts.

EASY

Quilt Size:	90" x 105"	
Block Size:	15"	
Blocks in Quilt:	42	

(21 pieced, 21 plain; 6 across by 7 down)

Material:
6-1/2 yds. White
1-1/2 yds. Solid for Unit B
Assorted Prints and Solids

Pieces per Block			per Quilt
A	1	White	21
B	8	Solid	168
C	16	Assorted	
		Print	336
D	32	White	672

in color p. 16

7. Beggar Block

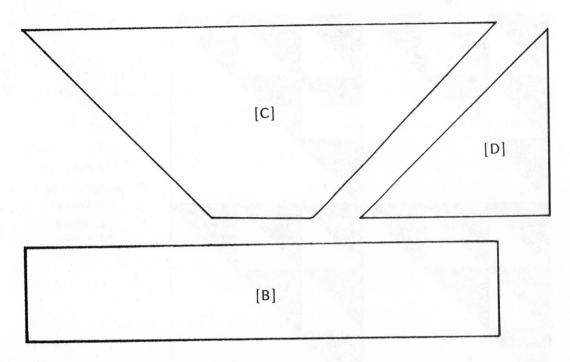

[C]

[D]

[B]

ADD 1/4" SEAM ALLOWANCE

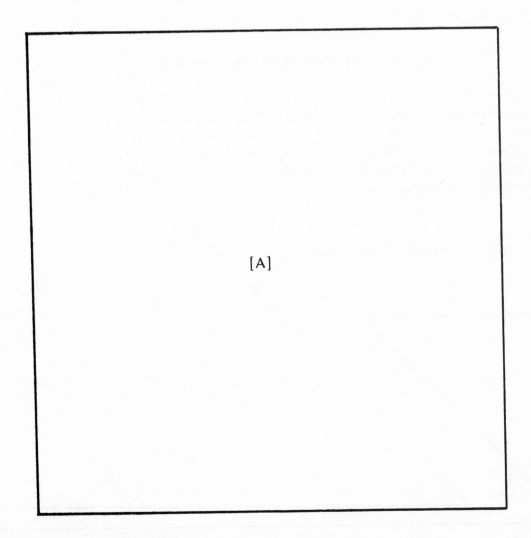

[A]

EASY

Quilt Size:	60" x 72"
Block Size:	12"
Blocks in Quilt:	30
	(5 across by 6 down)

Material:
  6-3/4 yds. White
  3-1/2 yds. Color

Pieces per Block			per Quilt
A	4	White	120
B	12	White	360
	24	Color	720

in color p. 8

8. Birds in the Air I

There are several versions of this pattern, which dates back to 1820.

    Sewing Instructions: To assemble the block, break it down into four smaller blocks, following the diagram. Each of these units will consist of a pieced half and a plain half.

    Border: A plain white border four inches wide can be added.

    Quilting: Quilt 1/8" from all seams. On the plain Pieces A, repeat the pieced design.

ADD 1/4" SEAM ALLOWANCE

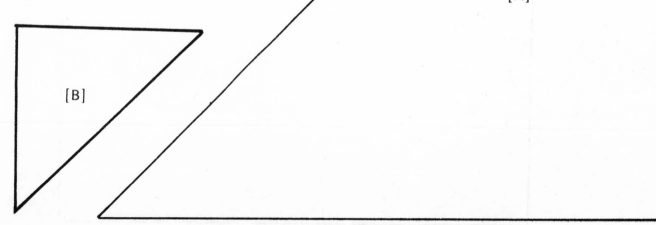

[A]

[B]

MODERATE

Quilt Size:	72" x 84"
Block Size:	12"
Blocks in Quilt:	42

   (21 pieced, 21 plain; 6 across by 7 down)

Material:
   5-1/2 yds. White
   Assorted Prints

Pieces per Block			per Quilt
A	4	White	84
B	80	Print	1680
	80	White	1680

in color p. 7

9. Birds in the Air II

This version of *Birds in the Air* also dates from at least 1820.

   Sewing Instructions: Visually break the block into three parts, a diagonal center strip and two large triangles. Then stitch Piece B, print and plain, into squares. Assemble the squares into strips and stitch these units to the two plain white triangles to make the large triangular units. Assemble the entire diagonal center strip. Finally, stitch the two corner triangles to each side of the center strip.

   Set blocks side by side. An over-all design, this quilt needs no border.

   Quilting: Quilt 1/8" from all seams.

ADD 1/4" SEAM ALLOWANCE

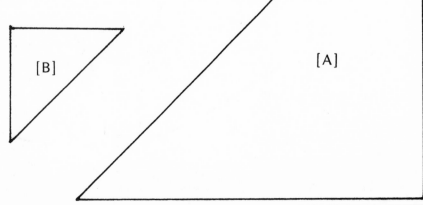

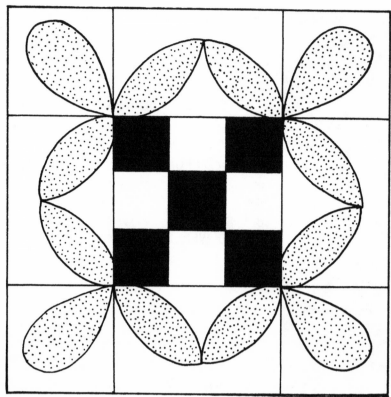

MODERATE

Quilt Size:	77" x 88"	
Block Size:	11"	
Blocks in Quilt:	56	
	(7 across by 8 down)	

Material:
7 yds. White
2-1/4 yds. Blue
For Honeybee:
1-1/2 yds. Gold
3/4 yds. Blue

Pieces per Block			**per Quilt**
A	4	White	224
B	4	White	224
C	4	White	224
	5	Blue	280
	5	Gold	*for Honeybee*
D	8	Blue	448
E	4	Blue	224
	4	Gold	*for Honeybee*

in color p. 8

10. Blue Blazes

Also known as *Honeybee.*

Sewing Instructions: This is a combined pieced and appliqued pattern. Piece the background block first, then applique parts D and E in place. Set blocks 7 across and 8 down.

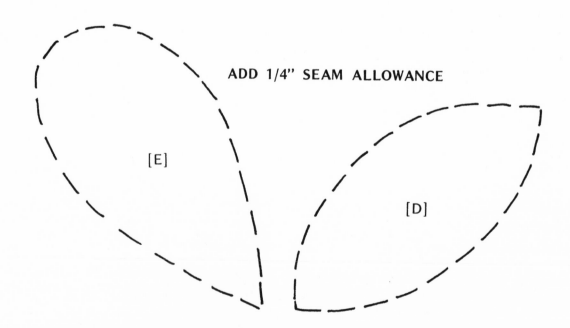

ADD 1/4" SEAM ALLOWANCE

[E]

[D]

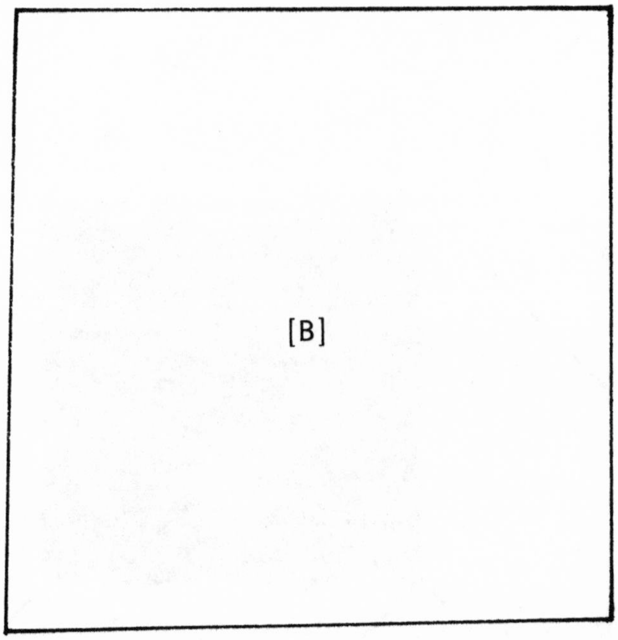

[B]

ADD 1/4" SEAM ALLOWANCE

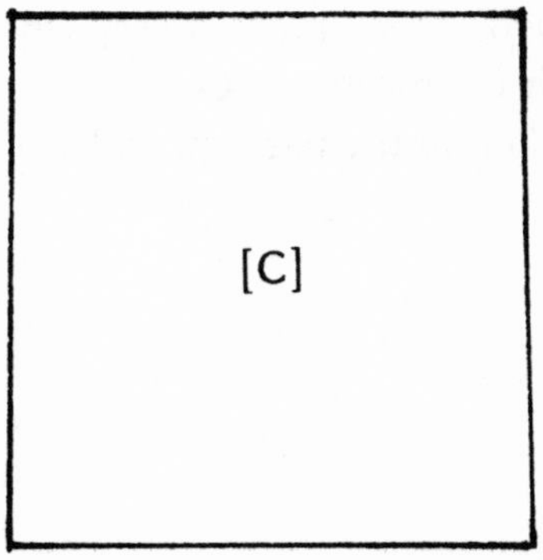

[C]

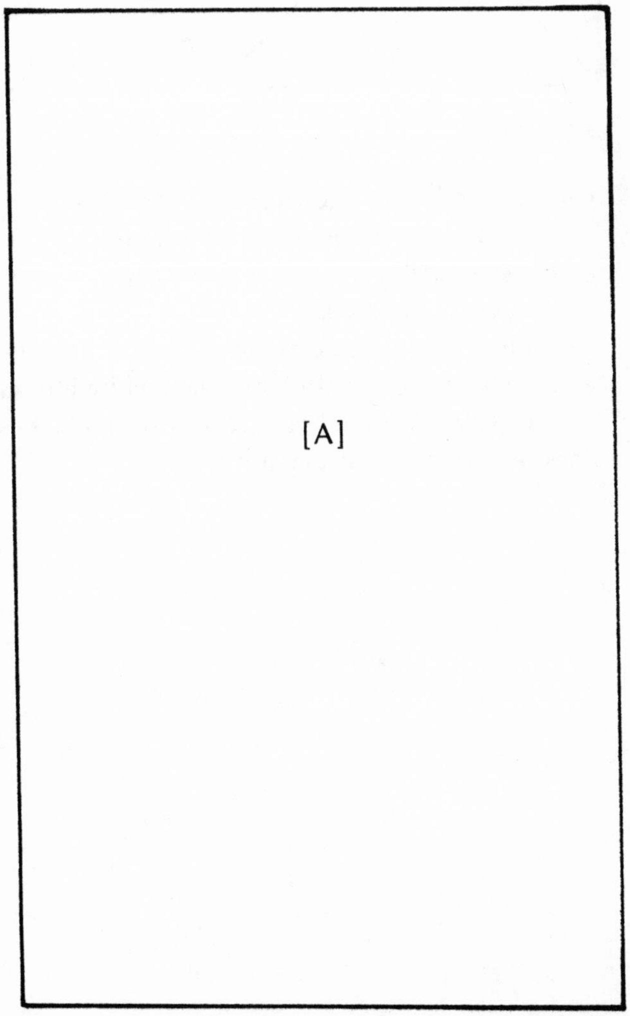

[A]

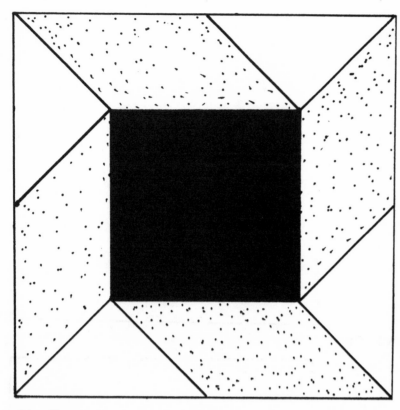

EASY

Quilt Size:	79-1/2" x 88-1/2"
Block Size:	9"
Blocks in Quilt:	72
	(8 across by 9 down)

Material:
4 yds. Red
3 yds. Blue
2-1/2 yds. White

Pieces per Block			per Quilt
A	1	Red	72
B	4	Blue	288
C	4	White	288

Other Units:
Border: 2 red strips, 4-1/4" x 80";
2 red strips, 4-1/4" x 89"

in color p. 6

11. Box

This pattern is also known as *Eccentric Star*.

Sewing Instructions: Cut out pattern pieces adding 1/4" seam allowance. To assemble block, start with center square. Stitch B to C and then to center. Continue around block until completed.

Blocks are set side by side with a red border added. Since this is a very vibrant quilt, you might choose to alternate plain white blocks with the pieced blocks.

Quilting: In the large areas, it would be best to ignore the pattern, and use diagonal lines or diamonds for the quilting.

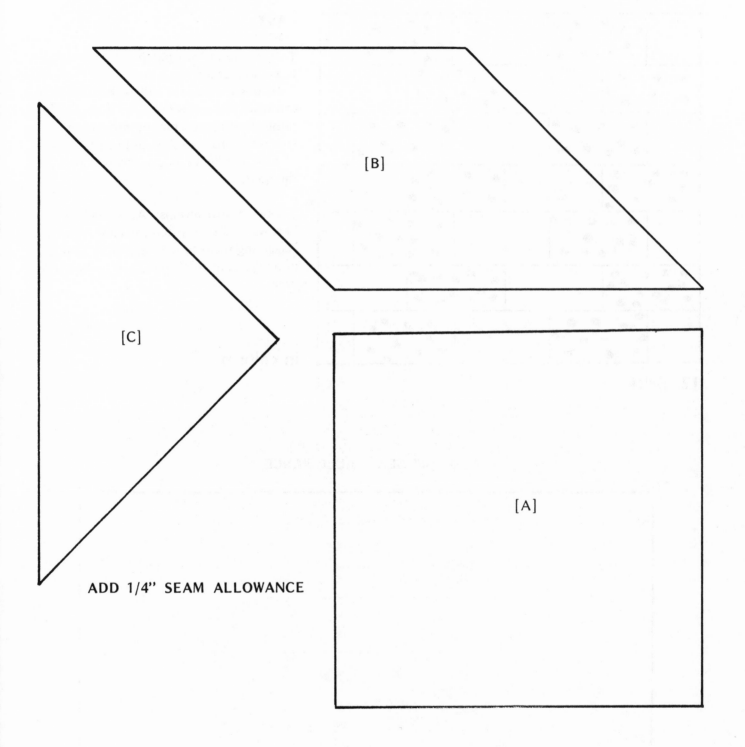

[B]

[C]

[A]

ADD 1/4" SEAM ALLOWANCE

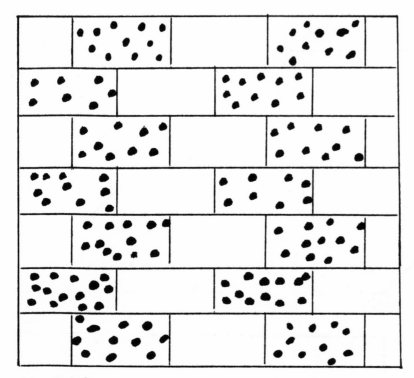

12. Brick

EASY

This is a simple one-patch design intended to be used as a scrap quilt.

Its possibilities are endless because you can work out a color scheme if you desire rather than using a hit-and-miss pattern. One way is to plan the quilt so that rows of dark and light run diagonally across the quilt.

Sewing Instructions: Assemble the top in rows, and then stitch the rows together, staggering them so they appear as in the drawing. Cut off the edges to make them even.

in color p. 3

ADD 1/4" SEAM ALLOWANCE

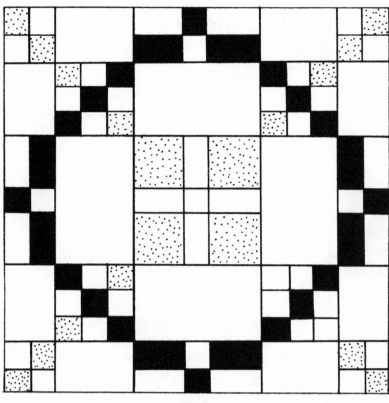

EASY

Quilt Size:	85" x 105"
Block Size:	15"
Blocks in Quilt:	20
	(4 across by 5 down)

Material:
5 yds. White
2-1/4 yds. Red
1 yd. Blue

Pieces		per Block	per Quilt
A	4	White	80
B	8	White	160
C	8	Blue	160
	12	White	240
D	4	Red	80
E	16	Blue	320
	16	Red	320
	29	White	580

Other Units:
Lattice Strips

13. Burgoyne Surrounded   in color p. 7

This pattern commemorates the surrender of General Burgoyne at the Battle of Saratoga in 1777, one of the most important events on the way to American independence. In 1850 the pattern became known as *Wheel of Fortune* and in 1860, in Ohio, *The Road to California*.

Sewing Instructions: Assemble the block as shown in the drawing. To join the blocks together, piece, using parts D and C (same as the center patch of the block). Cut a white strip 5" x 15"; join it to the completed block, and then set the blocks together using this strip to separate them.

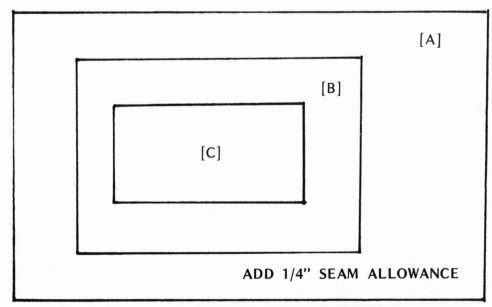

[A]
[B]
[C]
ADD 1/4" SEAM ALLOWANCE

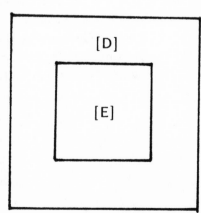

[D]
[E]

Lattice

DIFFICULT

Quilt Size:	84" x 84"
Block Size:	12"
Blocks in Quilt:	12
	(3 across by 4 down)

Material:
  6 yds. Orange
  4 yds. Gold
  3 yds. Green (Dark)

Pieces per Block			per Quilt
A	4	Orange	100
	2	Green	50
B	2	Green	50
C	1	Green	25

Other Units:
12 Gold Background Blocks, 12" square
     Lattice Strips, 3-1/2" x 12-1/2"
     3" Green Squares for corners

in color p. 13

14. Cactus Flower

A color illustration of this quilt, made in Pennsylvania about 1840, appears in *America's Quilts and Coverlets*. The background blocks are gold, with the flowers worked in orange and green. The lattice strips are orange, with a green square at each corner of the block. The outer edge is finished in green triangles, with a strip border in orange.

  Sewing Instructions: Piece the flowers and applique them to the gold background block. To assemble the top, begin with a quarter square in green, then a lattice strip with half of a 3"-square at each end. Add a flower block, with lattice strip on each side, joining a 3" green square at each end of the strip. Next, add a half triangle in green. Continue across the top of the quilt. The succeeding rows require half blocks on each edge, with flower blocks and lattice strips in between. Finish the bottom row in the same manner as the top.
  Border: Cut strips 6-1/2" wide, and stitch them around the quilt.
  Quilting: Quilt 1/8" on each side of the pieces. Use a filling stitch to complete the block with a cable for the lattice strips. A more elaborate design can be used for the border.

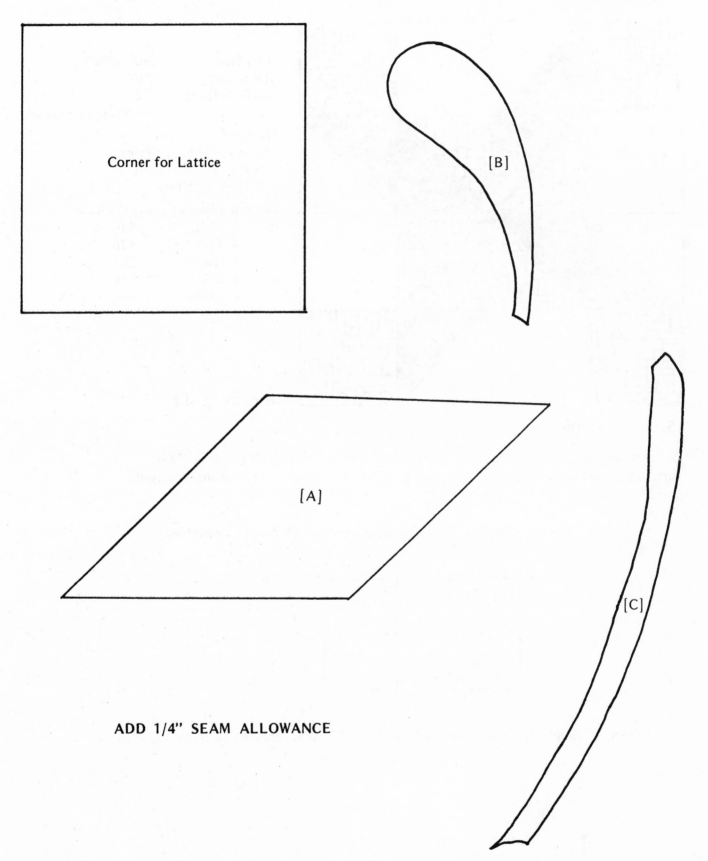

Corner for Lattice

[B]

[A]

[C]

ADD 1/4" SEAM ALLOWANCE

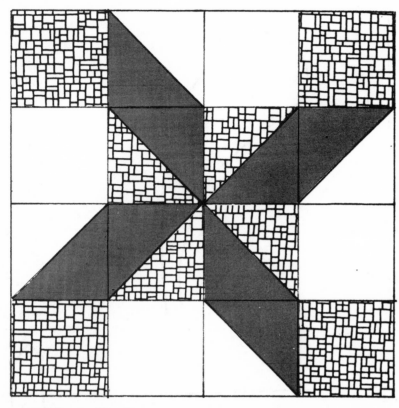

EASY

Quilt Size:	80" x 90"
Block Size:	10"
Blocks in Quilt:	72
	(8 across by 9 down)

Material:
  3-1/2 yds. Green Print
  6-1/2 yds. Red Print
  6-1/2 yds. White

Pieces per Block			per Quilt
A	4	White	576
	4	Red	576
B	4	Green	288
C	4	Red	576
	4	White	576

in color p. 14

15. Clay's Choice

Our pioneer grandmothers translated the events of their day into quilt patterns. This pattern honored Henry Clay. It has also been called *Harry's Star, Henry of the West,* and *Star of the West.*

Sewing Instructions: The following diagram shows how the block is assembled:

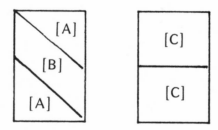

Border: A simple strip border, 3" to 4" wide, is all that is necessary to frame the quilt.

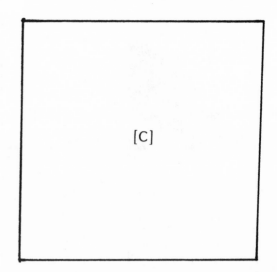

ADD 1/4" SEAM ALLOWANCE

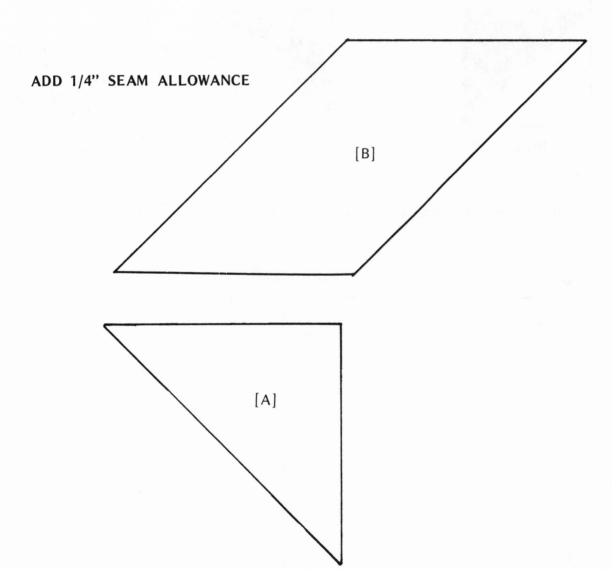

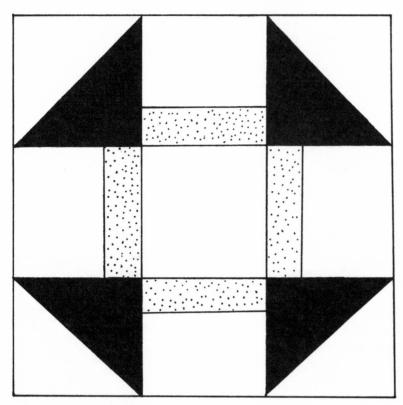

16. Churn Dash

EASY

Quilt Size:	90" x 101'
Block Size:	9"
Blocks in Quilt:	81
	(9 across by 9 down)

Material:
3 yds. White
3 yds. Color (Lattice Strips and Border)
Assorted Scraps

Pieces per Block			per Quilt
A	1	White	81
B	4	Dark	324
	4	White	324
C	4	Print	324
D	4	White	324

Other Units:
Lattice Strips, 2-1/2" x 10"
Border, 2 Color Strips, 2-1/2" x
90-1/2"; 2 Color Strips, 2-1/2" x
101-1/2"

in color p. 4

Although I cannot date this pattern, it must have been named for the old churn dashes used to make butter.

ADD 1/4" SEAM ALLOWANCE

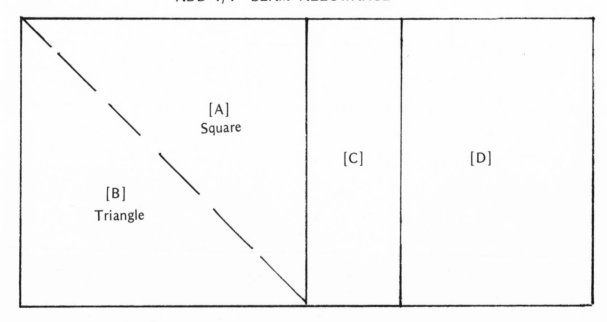

[A] Square

[B] Triangle

[C]

[D]

MODERATE

Quilt Size: 74" x 86"
Block Size: 12"
Blocks in Quilt: 42
    (21 pieced, 21 plain; 6 across by 7 down)

Material:
    5 yds. White
    2 yds. Yellow
    2 yds. Light Green

Pieces per Block		per Quilt
A	12 Green	
	20 White	
B	4 Yellow	
C	6 White	
	2 Yellow	

This pattern is also known as *Shoofly, Handy Andy, Hen and Chickens*, and *Duck and Ducklings*. The pattern we show for *Duck and Ducklings* has the same names, and is an alternate pattern for *Corn and Beans*.

in color p. 11

17. Corn & Beans

    Sewing Instructions: Cut out pattern pieces, adding 1/4" seam allowance. To assemble the block, start with the large middle square and work outward in rows.

    Border: Add a 2" border using one of the three colors used in the top.

    Quilting: Quilt 1/8" from all seams. On the plain blocks use a circular quilting design.

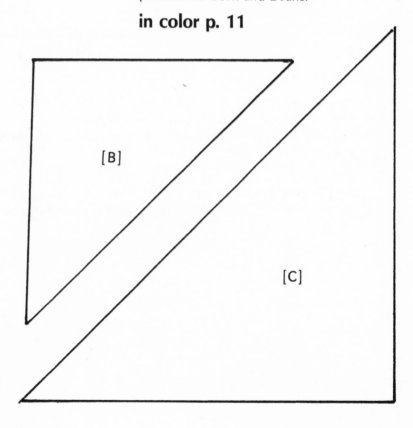

[B]

[C]

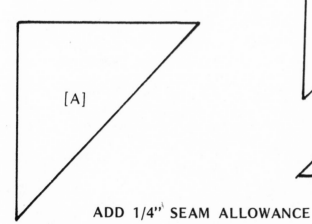

[A]

ADD 1/4" SEAM ALLOWANCE

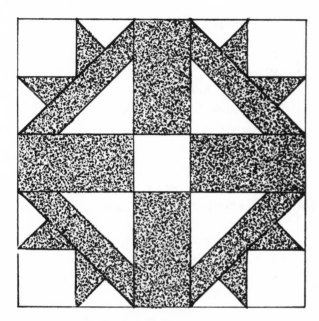

18. Cross & Crown

EASY

Quilt Size:	94″ x 94″
Block Size:	11″

Blocks in Quilt: 25
(5 across by 5 down)

Material:
15 yds. Color
13 yds. White

Pieces	per Block		per Quilt
A	4	White	100
B	8	White	200
C	16	Color	400
D	5	White	125
E	4	Color	100

Other Units:
40 Lattice Strips, 3″ x 13-3/4″
40 Color Squares, 3″
Border: (1) 4 Color Strips, 2-1/2″ x 76-3/4″; 4 Color Squares, 2-1/2″; for corners (2) 2 White Strips, 7-1/4″ x 80-3/4″; 2 White Strips, 7-1/4″ x 94-3/4″

in color p. 9

This pattern dates from Colonial days and, like all old patterns, has many variations. Below are shown three such variations, *Duck Paddle*, *Mexican Crown* and *Fannie's Fan*. The only difference in these patterns is the color arrangement. Everything else remains the same.

Sewing Instructions: Cut out pattern pieces, adding seam allowance, and follow the diagram. The blocks are set with lattice strips. There are two border strips.

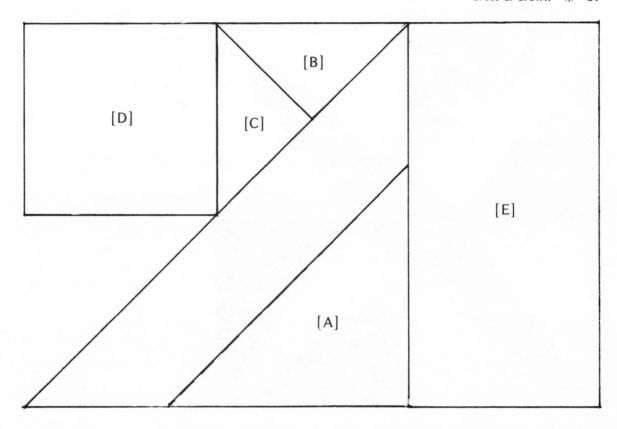

This pattern dates from Colonial days and, like all old patterns, has many variations. Below are shown three such variations, *Duck Paddle*, *Mexican Crown* and *Fannie's Fan*. The only difference in these patterns is the color arrangement. Everything else remains the same.

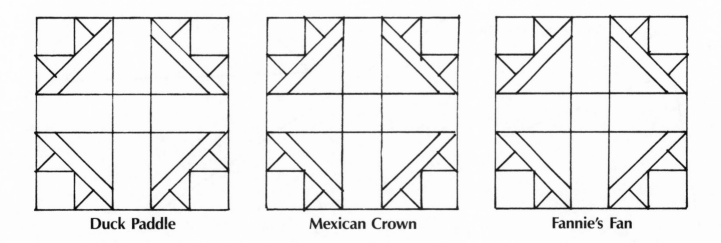

Duck Paddle   **Mexican Crown**   **Fannie's Fan**

EASY

Quilt Size:	84" x 96"
Block Size:	12"
Blocks in Quilt:	42
	(6 across by 7 down)

Material:
   6 yds. Dark Green, Print or Plain
   6 yds. Red or Gold, Print or Plain

Pieces	per Block		per Quilt
A	4	Dark Green	168
	4	Red	168
B	2	Dark Green	84
	2	Red	84
C	2	Dark Green	84
	2	Red	84

Other Units:
   Border: 2 Strips, 3-1/2" x 78-1/2";
      2 Strips 3-1/2" x 96-1/2"

in color p. 14

19. Crossed Canoes

Sewing Instructions: The blocks are assembled and joined side by side. A 6"-wide border is added at each edge. In a variation, you might cut 3" strips from each color.

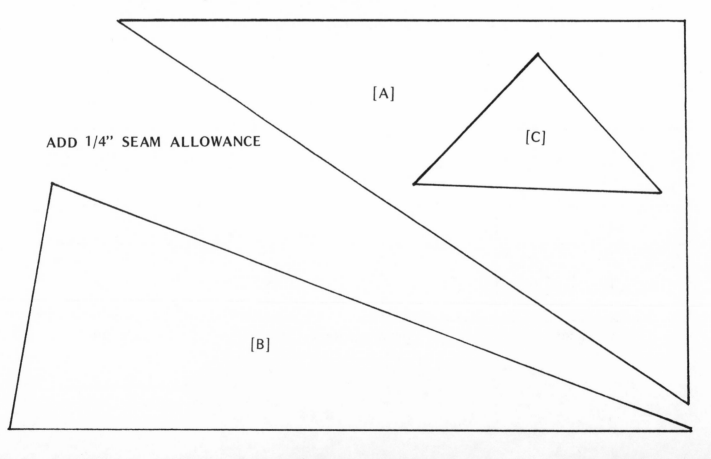

ADD 1/4" SEAM ALLOWANCE

[A]

[C]

[B]

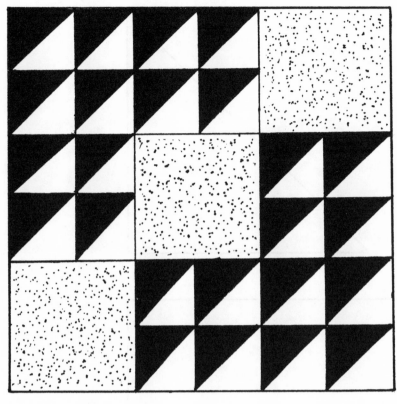

EASY

Quilt Size:	81" x 96"
Block Size:	15"
Blocks in Quilt:	30
	(5 across by 6 down)

Material:
  3 yds. White
  4-1/2 yds. Yellow
  5-1/2 yds. Orange

Pieces per Block			per Quilt
A	24	White	720
	24	Orange	720
B	3	Yellow	90

Other Units:
  Border: 2 Orange Strips, 3-1/2" x
    81-1/2"; 2 Orange Strips, 3-1/2"
    96-1/2"

in color p. 2

20. Cut Glass Dish

Sewing Instructions: Cut out pattern pieces, adding 1/4" seam allowance.
To assemble, stitch together one white and one orange triangle, Piece A, following drawing above. Make 24 per block. Then, for ease in joining the pieces, stitch together 6 blocks of 4 such units. Again, following the diagram, stitch these to Piece B.

Border: Cut out the 4" strips to the measurements given and stitch them to outer edges of quilt.

Quilting: Quilt 1/4" from each seam. The plain blocks can be quilted in a small circular motif, or the lines of quilting can be continued from the pieced sections into the plain blocks.

ADD 1/4" SEAM ALLOWANCE

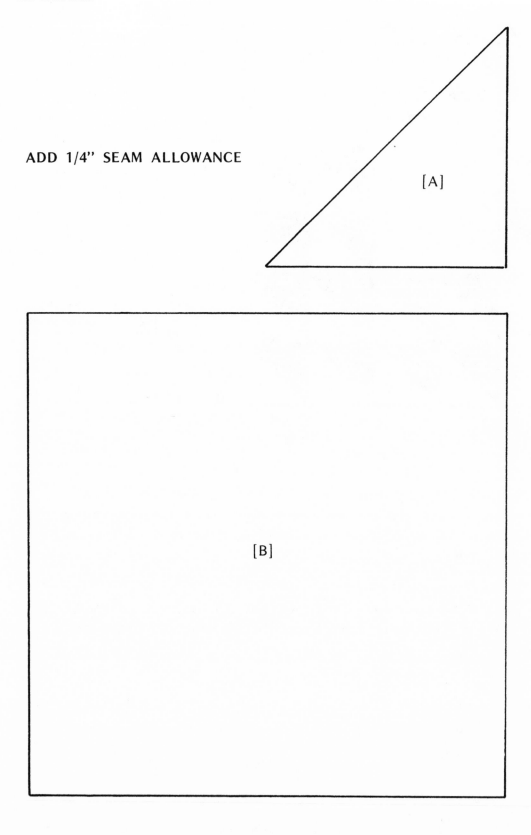

[A]

[B]

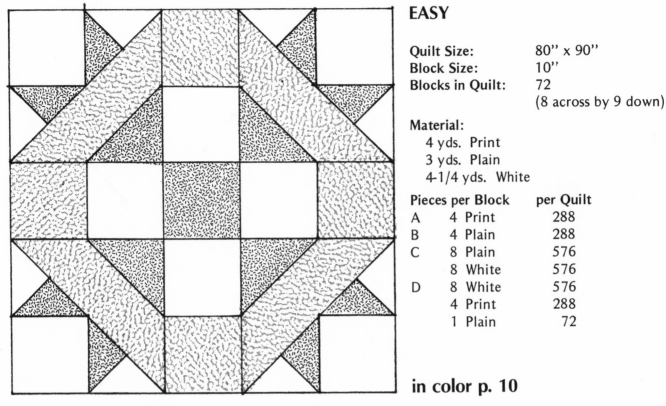

21. David & Goliath

EASY

Quilt Size:		80" x 90"
Block Size:		10"
Blocks in Quilt:		72
		(8 across by 9 down)

Material:
    4 yds. Print
    3 yds. Plain
    4-1/4 yds. White

Pieces per Block			per Quilt
A	4	Print	288
B	4	Plain	288
C	8	Plain	576
	8	White	576
D	8	White	576
	4	Print	288
	1	Plain	72

in color p. 10

This pattern has many names: *Four Darts, Bull's Eye, Flying Darts, Doe and Darts.*
It also bears a striking resemblance to the colonial pattern *Cross and Crown.*

Sewing Instructions: Cut out pattern units adding 1/4" seam allowance. To assemble, start with the four outer squares. Piece two plain C to two white C. Stitch these to a white D. Stitch print A to plain B and attach to the already completed unit. Assemble four of these for each block. For the center strips, stitch one print, one white, one plain, one white and one print using part D. Assemble side strips in same manner, omitting the center square. No border is necessary.

Quilting: Quilt 1/8" from all seams.

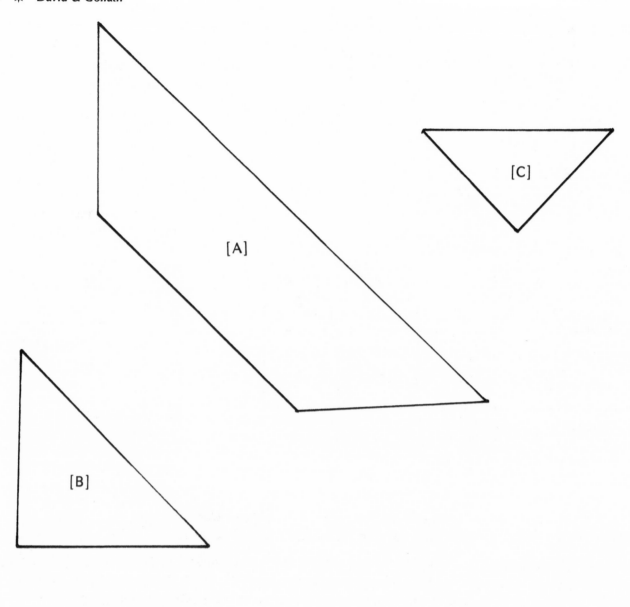

[C]

[A]

[B]

[D]

ADD 1/4" SEAM ALLOWANCE

22. Delectable Mountains   EASY   in color p. 9

This pattern originated in New England, inspired by John Bunyan's *Pilgrim's Progress*.
It dates back to early Colonial days and has long been a favorite with quiltmakers.
Usually it is made up in either blue or green and white. The blocks of mountains are
12'', and by adding succeeding rows, you can make a quilt of any desired size.

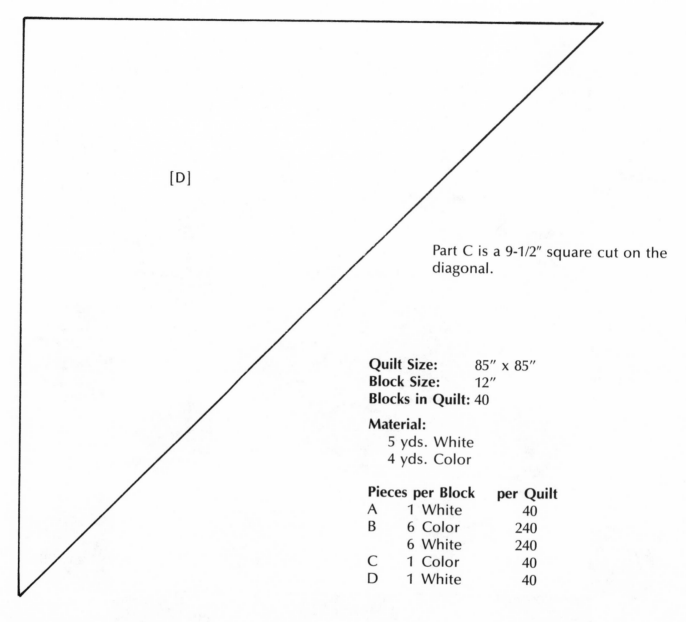

[D]

Part C is a 9-1/2″ square cut on the diagonal.

Quilt Size: 85″ x 85″
Block Size: 12″
Blocks in Quilt: 40

Material:
    5 yds. White
    4 yds. Color

Pieces	per Block		per Quilt
A	1	White	40
B	6	Color	240
	6	White	240
C	1	Color	40
D	1	White	40

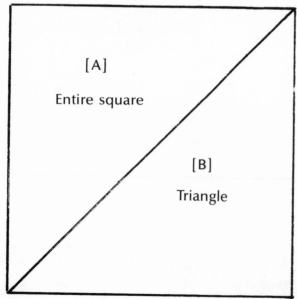

[A]

Entire square

[B]

Triangle

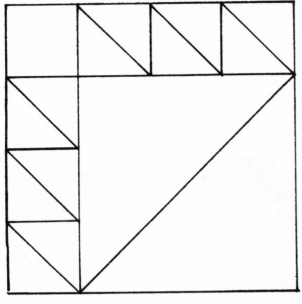

Block Diagram

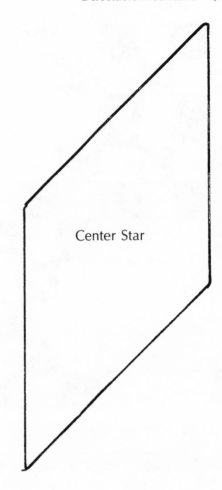

Center Star

For the center: Piece the star and 4 color units of the "Mountain," omitting the white part D. Sew these to the completed star center.

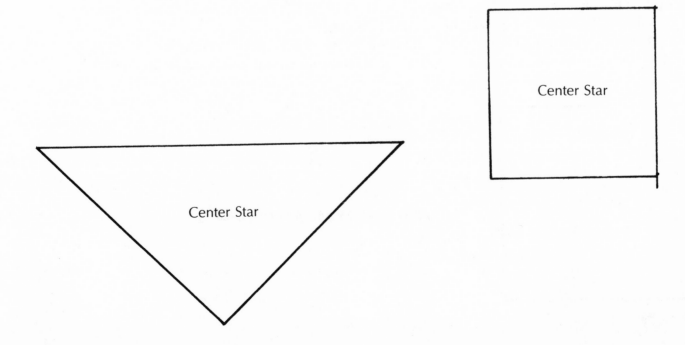

Center Star

Center Star

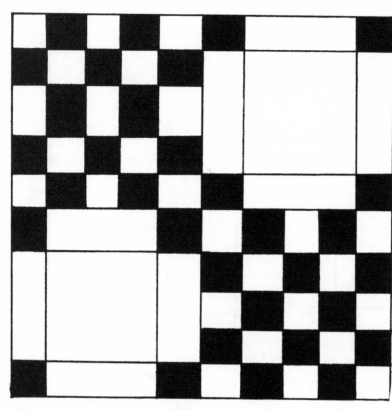

EASY

Quilt Size:		80" x 100"
Block Size:		20"
Blocks in Quilt:		20
		(4 across by 5 down)

Material:
   6 yds. White
   3-1/2 yds. Color

Pieces per Block			per Quilt
A	2	White	40
B	8	White	160
C	26	White	520
	32	Color	640

in color p. 5

23. Double Irish Chain

The *Double Irish Chain* dates from the middle 1800s. One reason for its continued popularity is its ease of assembly.

   Sewing Instructions: Cut out pattern pieces, adding 1/4" seam allowance. To assemble, break the block into four smaller squares, two blocks using Piece C, and two using Pieces A, B, and C.
   Border: No border is required. Just bind off the edges.
   Quilting: Elaborate quilting motifs — floral or circular — look good on the large squares. Or, alternatively, these center squares can be embellished with embroidered flowers.

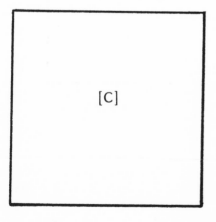

[C]

ADD 1/4" SEAM ALLOWANCE

[A]

[B]

24. Double T

EASY

Quilt Size: 78" x 93"
Block Size: 12"
Blocks in Quilt: 30
                (5 across by 6 down)

Material:
  7-1/2 yds. Color
  3 yds. White

Pieces per Block			per Quilt
A	1	Color	30
B	4	Color	120
C	16	Color	480
D	8	White	240

Other Units:
45 Lattice Strips, 12-1/2" x 3-1/2"
     3" Border Strips

in color p. 9

ADD 1/4" SEAM ALLOWANCE

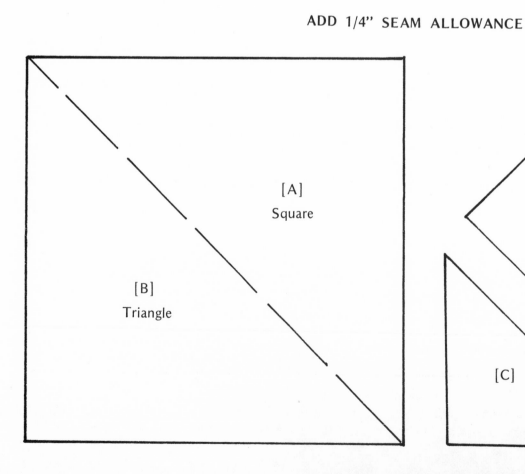

[A]
Square

[B]
Triangle

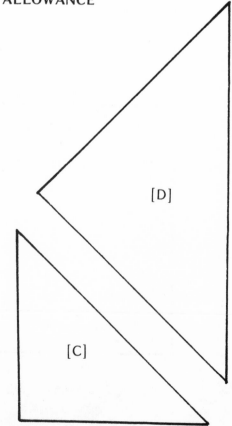

[D]

[C]

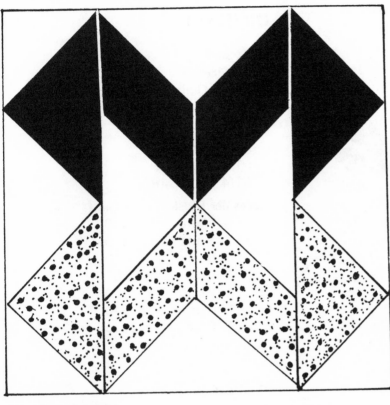

EASY

Quilt Size:	78" x 96"	
Block Size:	9"	
Blocks in Quilt:	80	
	(8 across by 10 down)	

Material:
- 7 yds. White
- 2-1/2 yds. Dark Color
- 2-1/2 yds. Light Color

Pieces	per Block	per Quilt
A	4 White	320
B	6 White	480
	2 Dark	160
	2 Light	160
C	2 Dark	160
	2 Light	160

Other Units:
> Border: 2 Strips, 3-1/2" x 78-1/2";
> 2 Strips, 3-1/2" x 96-1/2"

in color p. 9

25. Double Z

Double Z is also known as *Brown Goose*.

Sewing Instructions: The pattern is set with blocks side by side, eight across by ten down. It can also be made up as a scrap quilt set together with lattice strips. A 3" border goes around the edges.

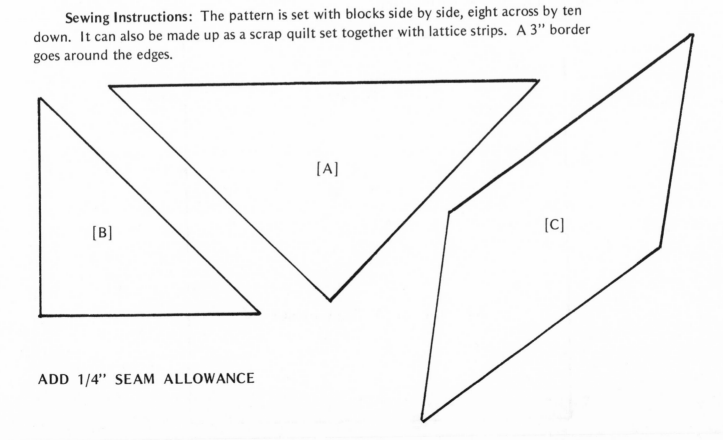

ADD 1/4" SEAM ALLOWANCE

26. Dove in the Window

DIFFICULT

Quilt Size:	70" x 84"	
Block Size:	14"	
Blocks in Quilt:	30	
	(5 across by 6 down)	

Material:
   1-1/4 yds. Blue
   1-1/4 yds. Rose
   7-1/4 yds. White

Pieces per Block			per Quilt
A	4	White	120
B	4	White	120
C	2	Blue	60
	2	Rose	60
	4	White	120
D	8	Blue	240
	8	Rose	240
	24	White	720

in color p. 7

Sewing Instructions: Cut out pattern pieces and assemble blocks following diagram. The blocks can also be set together with lattice strips.

[A]

ADD 1/4" SEAM ALLOWANCE

ADD 1/4" SEAM ALLOWANCE

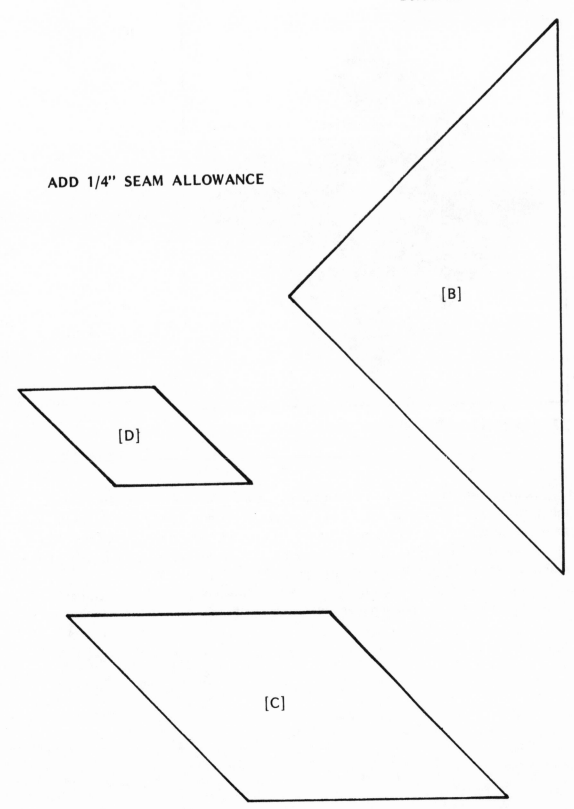

[B]

[D]

[C]

27. Fancy Dresden Plate

MODERATE

Quilt Size: 90" x 107"
Block Size: 17"
Blocks in Quilt: 30
(5 across by 6 down)

Material:
2-1/2 yds. Print or Plain (solid units)
7-1/2 yds. White (background blocks)
Assorted Prints & Solids

Pieces per Block			per Quilt
A	16	Assorted Prints	480
B	4	Print or Plain	120
C	4	Print or Plain	120
	1	18" White Square	30

Other Units:
Border: 2 Strips, 2-1/2" x 86";
2 Strips, 2-1/2" x 108"

in color p. 15

Sewing Instructions: Cut out design units, adding 1/4" seam allowance. Cut out thirty 18" squares for background. (The diagram shows only twelve printed pieces, but there are sixteen). Using the Center Diagram on page 52, mark the center of the block. This makes it easier to place the pieces properly. Lay down Piece C and then place Pieces A and B. When they are all properly arranged, stitch them down.

Quilting: A quilting diagram for the center is shown on page 52. The corners should be quilted with a filling pattern spaced one-half inch apart on the diagonal.

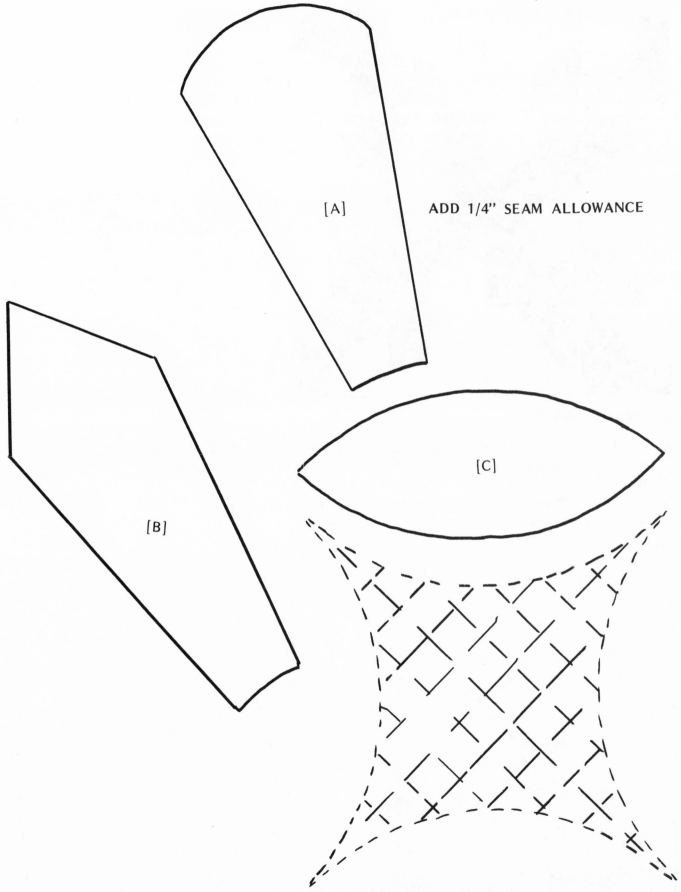

[A]

ADD 1/4" SEAM ALLOWANCE

[B]

[C]

MODERATE

Quilt Size:	80" x 96"
Block Size:	16"
Blocks in Quilt:	30
	(5 across by 6 down)

Material:
   5 yds. Dark Color
   5 yds. Light Color

Pieces per Block			per Quilt
A	8	Light	240
	8	Dark	240
B	8	Light	240
	8	Dark	240

in color p. 10

28. Drunkard's Path

This pattern dates back to 1849 or earlier. It is also known as *Rocky Road to Dublin, Rocky Road to California,* and *Country Husband.* It is usually made up in two colors, either red or blue and white.

   Sewing Instructions: Cut out pattern pieces and follow diagram.

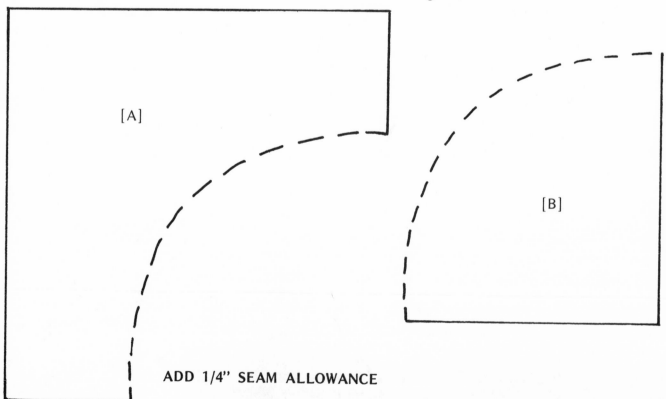

[A]

[B]

ADD 1/4" SEAM ALLOWANCE

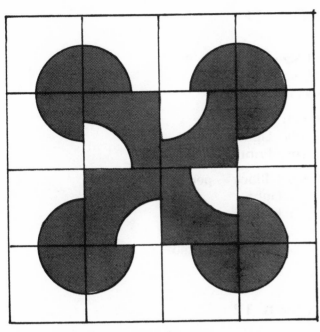

29. Wonder of the World

MODERATE

Quilt Size: 80″ x 96″
Block Size: 16″
Blocks in Quilt: 30

Material:
5-1/4 yds. White
3-1/2 yds. Dark

Pieces	per Block	per Quilt
A	12 White	360
	4 Dark	120
B	12 Dark	360
	4 White	120

in color p. 8

30. Fool's Puzzle

MODERATE

Quilt Size: 80″ x 96″
Block Size: 16″
Blocks in Quilt: 30

Material:
5 yds. Plain
5 yds. Print

Pieces	per Block	per Quilt
A	8 Plain	240
	8 Print	240
B	8 Plain	240
	8 Print	240

in color p. 12

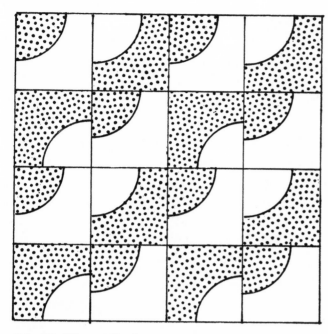

31. Falling Timbers

MODERATE

Quilt Size: 80" x 96"
Block Size: 16"
Blocks in Quilt: 30

Material:
   5 yds. Light
   5 yds. Print

Pieces per Block			per Quilt
A	8	Light	240
	8	Print	240
B	8	Light	240
	8	Print	240

in color p. 12

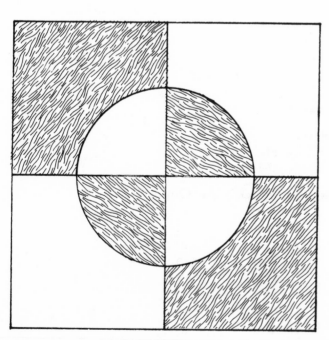

32. Vine of Friendship

MODERATE

Quilt Size: 72" x 80"
Block Size: 8"
Blocks in Quilt: 90

Material:
   3-1/4 yds. Print
   3-1/4 yds. Plain

Pieces per Block			per Quilt
A	2	Print	180
	2	Plain	180
B	2	Print	180
	2	Plain	180

in color p. 11

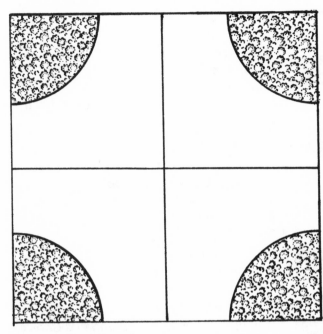

33. Mill Wheel

MODERATE

Quilt Size: 72″ x 80″
Block Size: 8″
Blocks in Quilt: 90

Material:
    4-1/2 yds. Plain
    2 yds. Print

Pieces	per Block	per Quilt
A	4 Plain	360
B	4 Print	360

in color p. 6

34. No Name

MODERATE

Quilt Size: 80″ x 96″
Block Size: 16″
Blocks in Quilt: 30

Material:
    5 yds. Light Fabric
    5 yds. Dark Fabric

Pieces	per Block	per Quilt
A	8 Light	240
	8 Dark	240
B	8 Light	240
	8 Dark	240

in color p. 5

EASY

Quilt Size:	80-1/2" x 92"
Block Size:	11-1/2"
Blocks in Quilt:	56
	(7 across by 8 down)

Material:
  4 yds. White
  3-1/4 yds. Color

Pieces	per Block		per Quilt
A	1	Color	56
B	4	White	224
C	12	White	672
	4	Color	224
D	4	Color	224

This pattern dates from colonial days. It is also known as *Grandmother's Choice, Handy Andy, Corn & Beans, Hens & Chickens,* and *Wild Goose Chase.*

in color p. 10

35. Duck & Ducklings

Sewing Instructions: Cut out pattern pieces and follow the diagram.

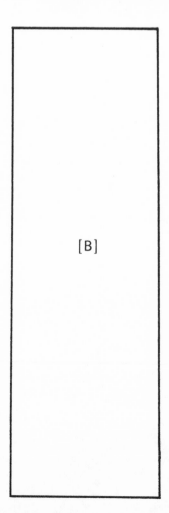

[B]

[A]

[C]

[D]

ADD 1/4" SEAM ALLOWANCE

MODERATE

Quilt Size:	80" x 100"	
Block Size:	10"	
Blocks in Quilt:	80	
	(8 across by 10 down)	

Material:
  3 yds. Dark Color
  8 yds. White or Light Color

Pieces per Block			per Quilt
A	1	White	80
B	2	Dark	160
C	2	White	160

in color p. 5

36. Drunkard's Trail

Apparently this is a rather old pattern, but I can't date it. It will make up quite well in any two colors, dark and light, and is simple to put together.

Sewing Instructions: Cut out pattern pieces, adding 1/4" seam allowance. To assemble the block, stitch one Piece B to one Piece C. Make two such units and then stitch these to Piece A.

Setting the Quilt: Follow the diagram on page 60 to set the blocks together.

Border: Bind the edges of the assembled quilt with a dark binding.

Quilting: Quilt along each seam line, 1/8" from the seam.

ADD 1/4" SEAM ALLOWANCE

[A]

PLACE ON FOLD
HALF PATTERN

[B]

[C]

Diagram for Setting Drunkard's Trail

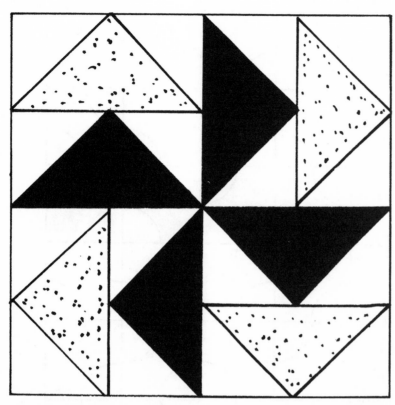

EASY

Quilt Size:	84" x 96"
Block Size:	12"
Blocks in Quilt:	56

   (28 pieced, 28 plain; 7 across by 8 down)

Material:
   1-1/4 yds. Red
   1-1/4 yds. Yellow
   6-1/2 yds. White

Pieces per Block			per Quilt
A	16	White	448
B	4	Red	112
	4	Yellow	112

in color p. 4

37. Dutchman's Puzzle

Sewing Instructions: Cut out pattern pieces and follow diagram. The top is set together with alternate plain blocks.

ADD 1/4" SEAM ALLOWANCE

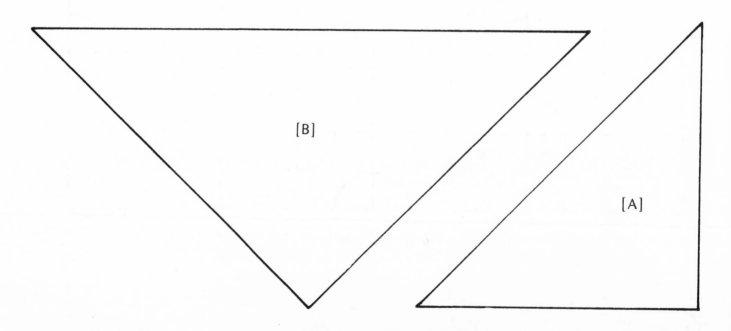

38. Dusty Miller

DIFFICULT

Quilt Size: 78" x 93"
Block Size: 12"
Blocks in Quilt: 30
                         (5 across by 6 down)

Material:
    1-3/4 yds. Brown
    3-3/4 yds. Gold Print
    5-1/2 yds. White

Pieces	per Block		per Quilt
A	1	Gold	30
B	4	White	120
C	4	Gold	120
D	4	White	120
E	8	Brown	240
F	4	White	120
G	8	Brown	240
H	4	White	120
I	8	Brown	240
J	4	White	120
K	8	Brown	240
L	4	White	120

Other Units:
45   Lattice Strips, 3-1/2" x 12-1/2"
       Border: 2 Strips, 3-1/2" x 72-1/2";
          2 Strips, 3-1/2" x 93-1/2"

in color p. 3

This pattern dates from the early 1800s.

   Sewing Instructions: Cut out pattern pieces, adding 1/4" seam allowance. Stitch together Pieces D through K, and then join to Piece L. Join Pieces B and C. Then join these completed units and add the center circle to form the block. Join the completed blocks with the lattice strips.
   Border: Cut 3-1/2" strips and join them to the outside edges.
   Quilting: Quilt 1/8" from all seams of the pieced blocks. Quilt the lattice strips and border with a rope or feather design.

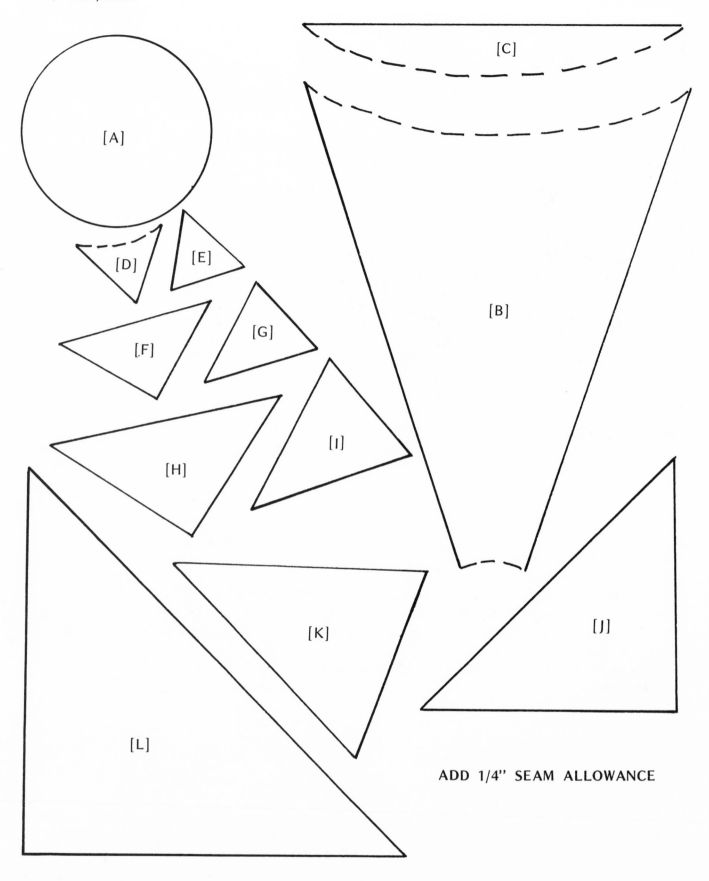

[A]

[C]

[B]

[D]

[E]

[F]

[G]

[H]

[I]

[K]

[J]

[L]

ADD 1/4" SEAM ALLOWANCE

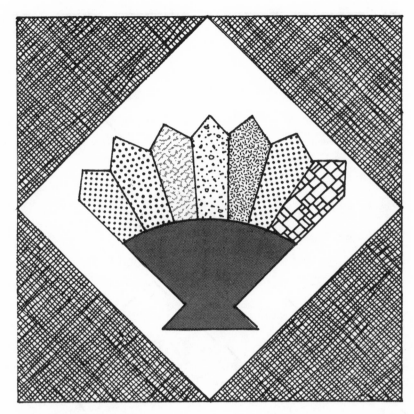

39. Dobbin's Fan

EASY

Quilt Size:		85" x 85"
Block Size:		20"
Blocks in Quilt:		13

(9 worked, 4 background;
3 across by 3 down)

Material:

8 yds. Small Pastel Floral Print
(background)

2 yds. White
1 yd. Solid Color (bottom of fan)
Assorted Scraps

Pieces	per Block		per Quilt
A	1	Solid Color	9
B	7	Assorted Prints	63
C	4	Floral Print	36
	1	14" White Square	9

Other Units:

4 Background Blocks, 20" square
8 Half Squares
4 Quarter Squares

in color p. 6

This pattern dates from the early 1800s.

Sewing Instructions: Cut out units for each block, allowing 1/4" seam allowance. Cut out a 14" white square (pattern not shown), adding 1/4" seam allowance. You will need nine of these squares. Also cut out four 20" squares of the background print, eight half squares and four quarter squares (patterns not shown).

Stitch a Piece C to each side of the white square to form the block. Applique Piece A in place, leaving the top free. Lay down and stitch Pieces B in place; then stitch down the top of Piece A. This completes the block.

To set the blocks together, stitch a quarter block to a completed block. Add a half block, another worked block, a half block, a worked block, and a quarter square. This completes the first row. The second row starts with a half block, a plain block, a plain block, a half block. Continue in this manner until the quilt is set together.

Border: Bind off the edges of the quilt.

Quilting: Since the background is a print, we recommend that the quilting be straight lines of stitching 1/4" apart. Outline the pattern units.

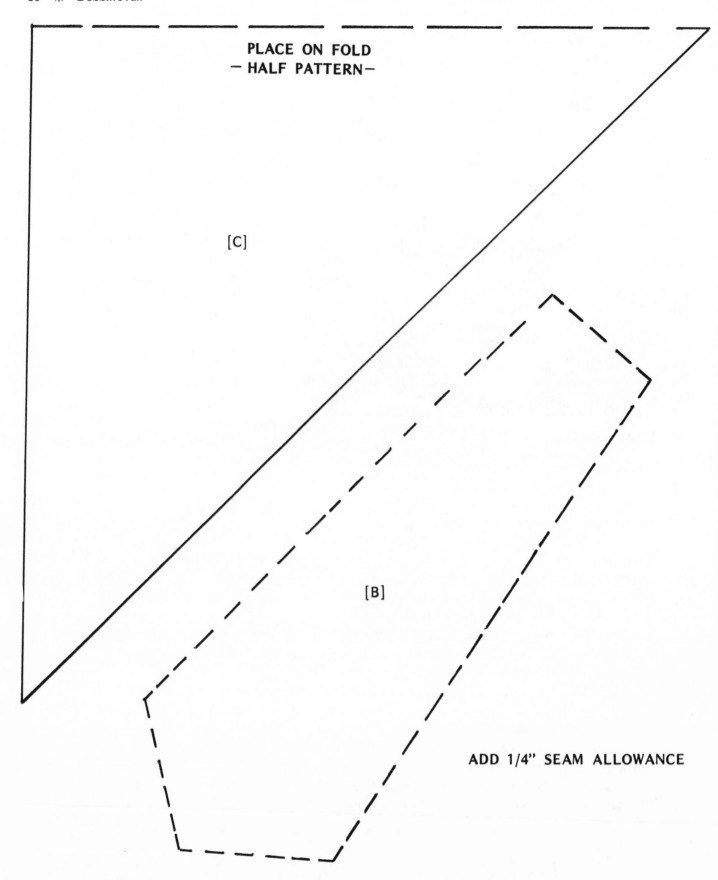

PLACE ON FOLD
— HALF PATTERN—

[C]

[B]

ADD 1/4" SEAM ALLOWANCE

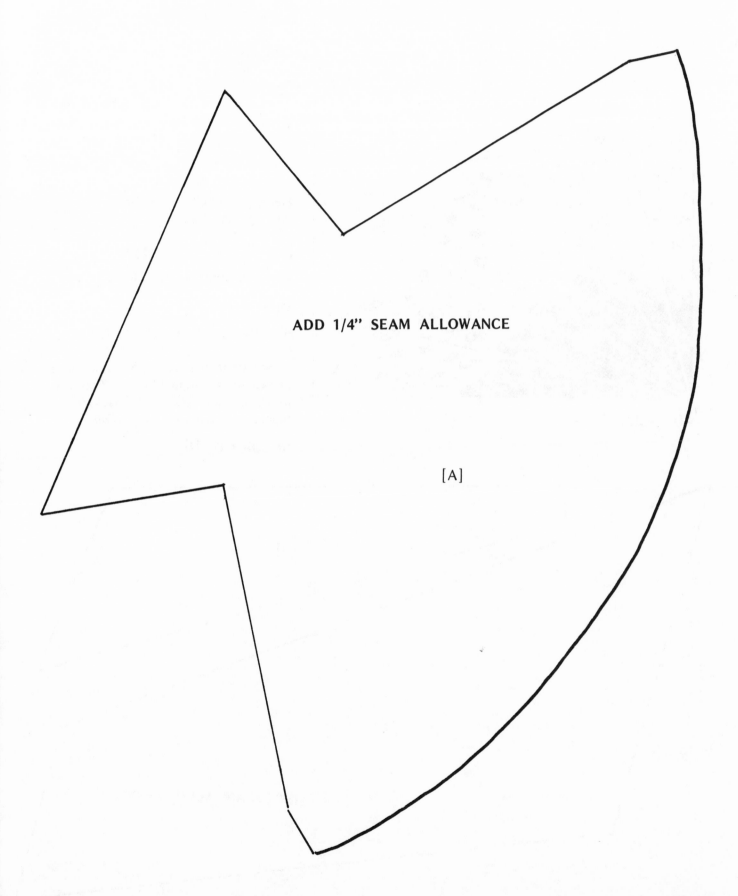

ADD 1/4" SEAM ALLOWANCE

[A]

40. Milady's Fan

MODERATE

Quilt Size:	84" x 98"
Block Size:	14"
Blocks in Quilt:	42
	(6 across by 7 down)

Material:
  8 yds. White
  Assorted scraps
  2-1/4 yds. Plain Color

Pieces per Block		per Quilt
A	6 Assorted	
	Prints	252
B	6 Color	252

42 background blocks, 14-1/2" x 14-1/2"

Other Units:

42 Background Blocks, 14-1/2" square

Sewing Instructions: A combination pieced and appliqued block. Piece the fan parts, then applique to the background block. (See *Grandmother's Fan.*)

in color p. 16

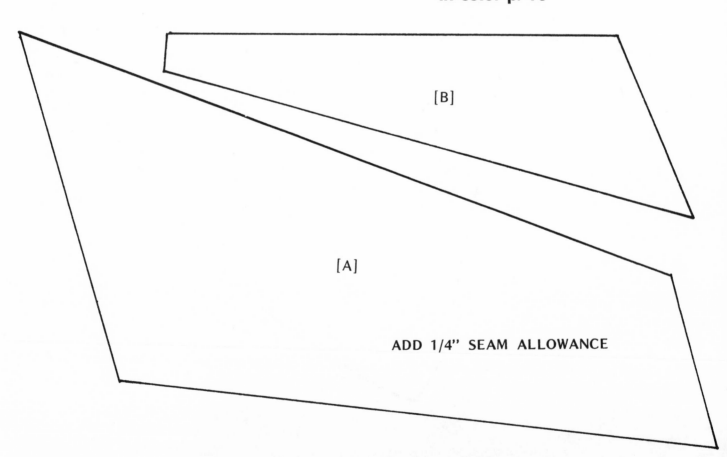

[B]

[A]

ADD 1/4" SEAM ALLOWANCE

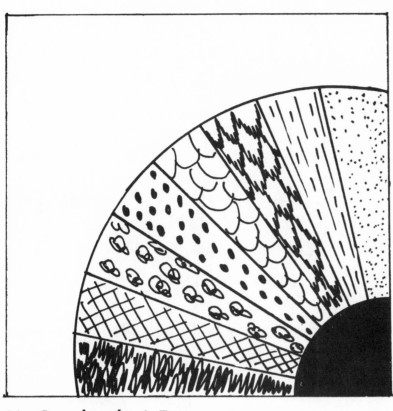

EASY

Quilt Size:	72" x 84"
Block Size:	12"
Blocks in Quilt:	42
	(6 across by 7 down)

Material:
5-1/2 yds. White
Assorted Scraps

Pieces per Block			per Quilt
A	1	Plain Color	42
B	8	Assorted	
		Print and	
		Plain	336

Other Units:
42   Background Blocks, 12" square

in color p. 15

41. Grandmother's Fan

This is an all-time favorite pattern, possibly because it utilizes so many odds and ends of fabrics. In the past, silks and woolens were frequently used.

Sewing Instructions: The fan is first pieced as shown, then appliqued to a background block, 12-1/2" square. Some designs show the fan with six segments, and some show it, as we have, with eight. The completed blocks are set side by side in rows, six across and seven down.

Border: A very pretty effect can be created by appliqueing the fan shapes onto a 12"-wide strip to form a border, but a border is optional.

ADD 1/4" SEAM ALLOWANCE

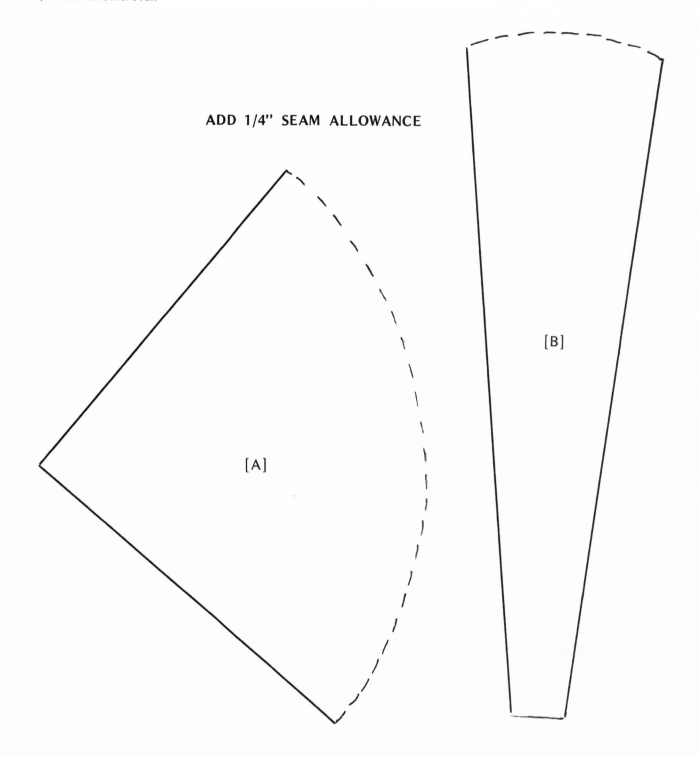

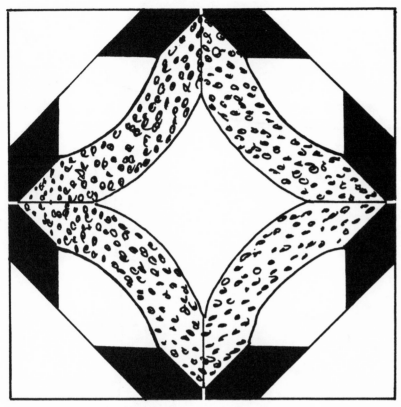

42. Friendship Knot

MODERATE

Quilt Size:		98" x 114"
Block Size:		16"
Blocks in Quilt:		30
		(5 across by 6 down)

Material:
   9 yds. Yellow
   4-1/2 yds. Red Print
   2-1/4 yds. Black Print

Pieces per Block			per Quilt
A	1	Yellow	30
B	4	Red	120
C	4	Yellow	120
		(Reverse half before cutting)	
D	8	Black	240
E	4	Yellow	120

Other Units:
   Border: 2 Yellow Strips, 9-1/4" x 99";
               2 Yellow Strips, 9-1/4" x 115"

in color p. 4

This pattern is also known as *Starry Crown.*

   Sewing Instructions: Cut out pattern parts, adding 1/4" seam allowance. To assemble the block, join 4 Pieces B, end to end, then join to Piece A.   Join Piece C to each Piece D. Add Piece E to each corner to complete block.

   Border: Stitch the 99" strips to the top and bottom and the 115" strips to each side to finish. Cut out 1-3/4" red bias strips for binding.

   Quilting: Outline each pattern piece 1/4" from seams. On the border use a cable pattern along the outside edges and straight quilting lines from the quilt top to the outside cable stitch.

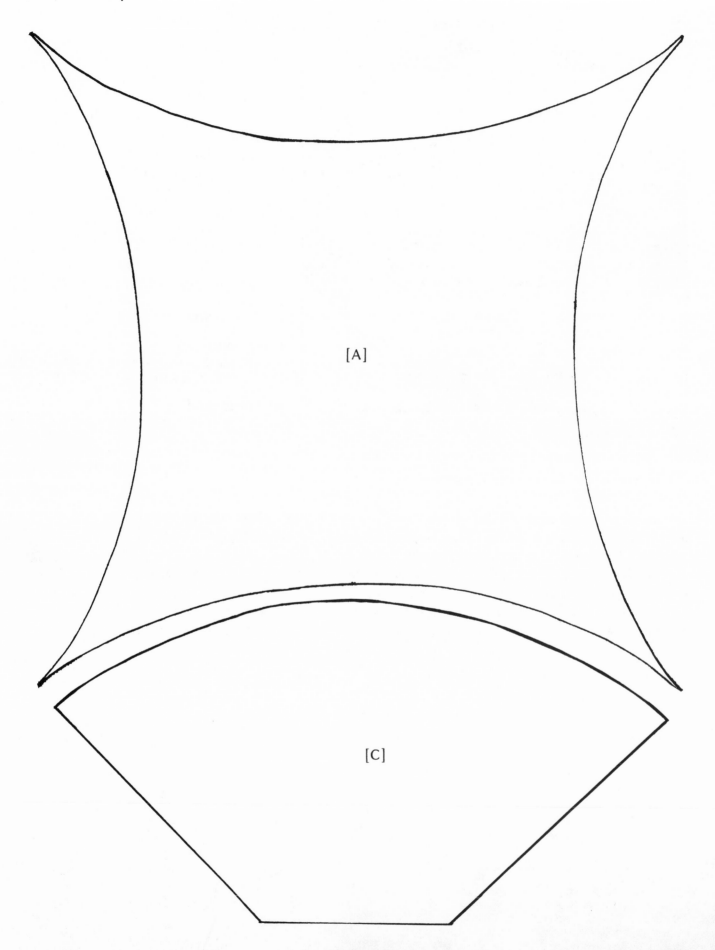

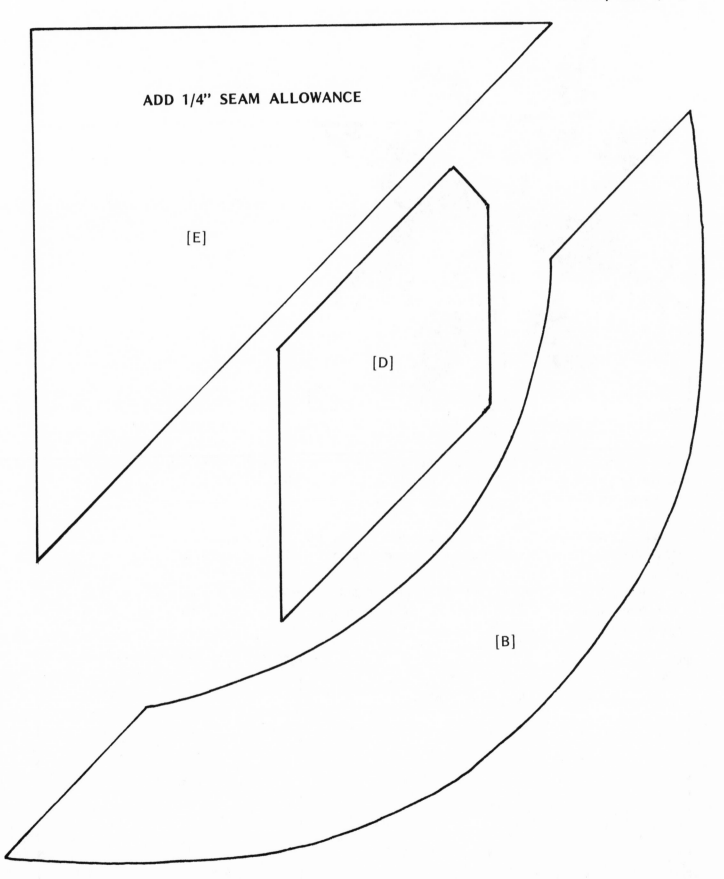

ADD 1/4" SEAM ALLOWANCE

[E]

[D]

[B]

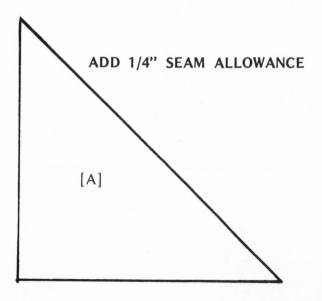

EASY

Quilt Size:	77" x 77"
Block Size:	11"
Blocks in Quilt:	49
	(7 across by 7 down)

Material:
    5-1/3 yds. Print
    7 yds. White

	Pieces per Block	per Quilt
A	12 Print	588
	12 White	588
B	4 White	196

in color p. 5

43. Barbara Frietchie Rose

Barbara Frietchie, born in 1766, was the subject of the poem by Whittier. The Frietchie House in Frederick, Maryland, is open to the public, and the original quilt using this pattern can be seen there.

    Sewing Instructions: This is an easy pattern to piece, since each block, with the exception of the corner squares, is assembled from Piece A and stitched together following the diagram.

    If lattice strips are used between the blocks, the quilt can be made up as a scrap quilt. If the corner squares are divided diagonally and pieced in print and plain, this pattern becomes *Star Puzzle.*

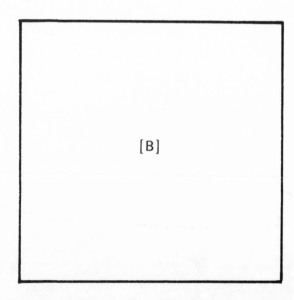

ADD 1/4" SEAM ALLOWANCE

[A]

[B]

44. Garden Path

EASY

Quilt Size:	69" x 90"
Block Size:	21"
Blocks in Quilt:	12
	(3 across by 4 down)

Material:
  6 yds. White
  5 yds. Solid (path)
  4 yds. Assorted Prints

Pieces per Block			per Quilt
A	8	Print	96
B	8	Print	96
	20	Solid	240
	28	White	336

in color p. 9

This lovely pattern uses up many odds and ends of scraps.

   Sewing Instructions: Cut out pattern pieces, adding 1/4" seam allowance. Assemble the blocks by following the diagram above.
   Border: When the quilt is finished, add a 3" strip border to edges.
   Quilting: Quilt 1/8" from all seam lines.

[A]

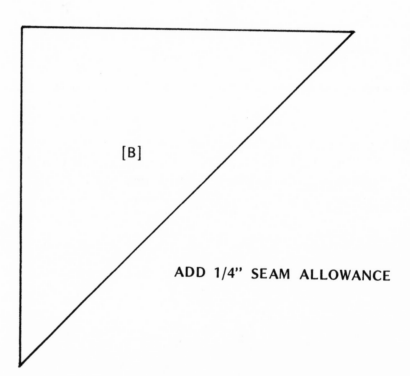

[B]

ADD 1/4" SEAM ALLOWANCE

45. Golden Gate

EASY

Quilt Size:	89-1/2" x 102"	
Block Size:	7-1/2" with 2" strips set	
Blocks in Quilt:	56	
	(7 across by 8 down)	

Material:
  2 yds. Yellow or Gold
  1 yd. Brown Print
  1 yd. Brown
  6 yds. for Lattice Strips and Other Units

	Pieces per Block		per Quilt
A	4	Yellow	224
	4	Brown Print	224
B	4	Yellow	224
	8	Brown	448
C	1	Yellow	56

Other Units:
	Lattice Strips
26	Half Blocks
4	Quarter Blocks

in color p. 11

This is a variation of a simple nine patch. Another name for this pattern is *Puss in the Corner.*

    Sewing Instructions: Cut out pattern units, adding 1/4" seam allowance. This is an easy block to stitch together. Divide it into its nine patches, and just stitch them as shown. You have four diagonal patches and four striped patches set around a plain center patch.

    Setting the Quilt: The blocks are set diagonally using lattice strips. Stitch a 2"-wide lattice strip to a block, and join it diagonally to the next block. Assemble these strips in rows. To finish you may leave the pointed ends as a border, or fill them in with half blocks cut from the lattice material, using a quarter block for each corner.

    Quilting: Quilt 1/8" from all seams. Use a circular pattern for the center of each block.

ADD 1/4" SEAM ALLOWANCE

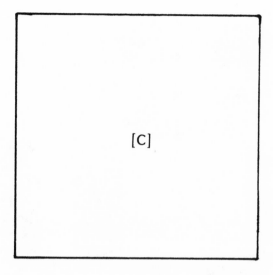

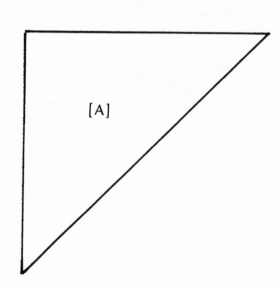

[C]

[B]

[A]

46. Flying Geese

EASY

Quilt Size:	78" x 93"	
Block Size:	12"	
Blocks in Quilt:	30	
	(5 across by 6 down)	

Material:
   7 yds. White
   3-3/4 yds. Color

Pieces per Block			per Quilt
A	4	White	120
B	1	Color	30
C	16	White	480
	16	Color	480

Other Units:
   Lattice Strips, 3-1/2" x 12-1/2"
   Border Strips, 3-1/2" wide

in color p. 6

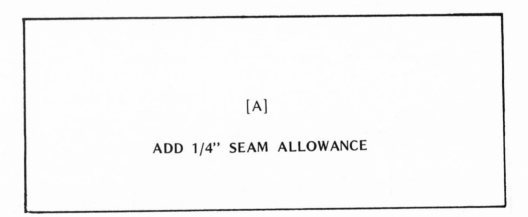

[A]

ADD 1/4" SEAM ALLOWANCE

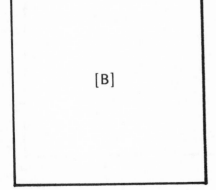

[B]

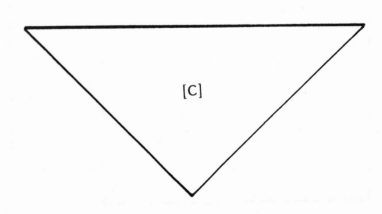

[C]

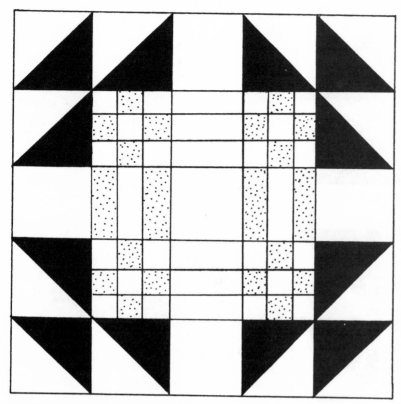

47. Goose in the Pond

EASY

Quilt Size:	75" x 81"
Block Size:	15"
Blocks in Quilt:	16

(64 across by 4 down)

Material:
1-1/2 yds. Green
2-1/2 yds. Gold
6 yds. White

Pieces per Block		per Quilt
A	5 White	80
B	12 Green	192
	12 White	192
C	8 Gold	128
	4 White	64
D	16 Gold	256
	20 White	320

Other Units:
24 Lattice Strips, 3-1/2" x 15-1/2"
 9 3" Squares
    Border: 2 Strips, 3-1/2" wide;
       2 Strips, 6-1/2" wide

in color p. 11

Sewing Instructions: Cut out pattern pieces and follow diagram. To set the quilt together you will need 24 lattice strips, 15-1/2" x 3-1/2", with a 3" nine-patch square at each intersection. There is a 3" border at sides and a 6" border at top and bottom.

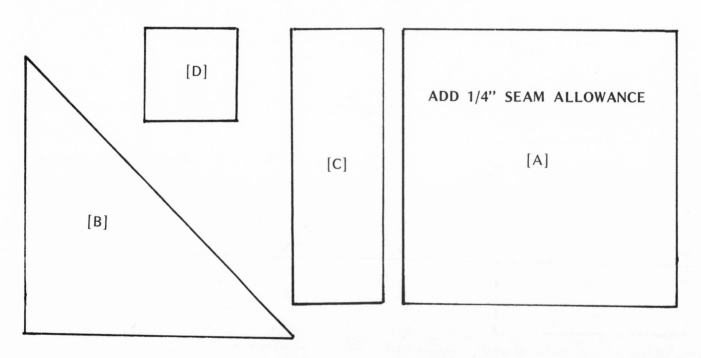

[D]

[C]

ADD 1/4" SEAM ALLOWANCE

[A]

[B]

48. Grandmother's Flower Garden

DIFFICULT

This pattern has long been a favorite among quiltmakers. It uses up huge quantities of small scrap pieces.

Because this is a scrap quilt, neither yardages nor sizes have been given.

Sewing Instructions: The blocks are made up of a center in a solid color, the next row in scrap prints, and the outer row in white or a harmonizing pastel to form rows through the flower garden. Just keep adding blocks until the top is the size you want.

in color p. 10

ADD 1/4" SEAM ALLOWANCE

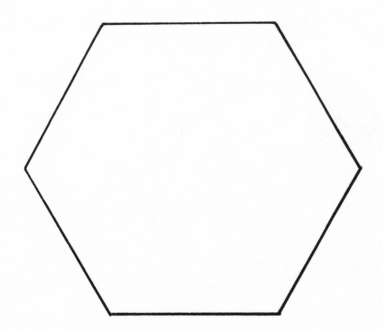

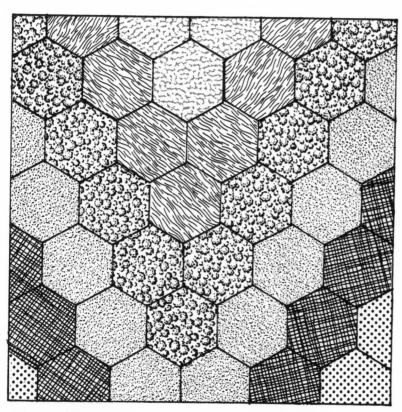

49. Ocean Wave I

DIFFICULT

The two patterns given here use the same pattern piece as *Grandmother's Flower Garden*.

Ocean Wave is also a scrap quilt, assembled in rows. The recurring color, as shown by the dark row, repeated throughout the design, produces the *Ocean Wave* pattern.

in color p. 16

50. Honeycomb

DIFFICULT

To assemble this design, begin at the center and work toward the edges in succeeding rows. This is also a scrap pattern with every other row in a solid color.

in color p. 16

51. Hands All Around

MODERATE

Quilt Size:		70" x 84-1/2"
Block Size:		14-1/2"
Blocks in Quilt:		20
		(4 across by 5 down)

Material:
   2-3/4 yds. White
   2 yds. Print
   4 yds. Dark Color

Pieces per Block			per Quilt
A	1	White	20
B	4	Print	80
C	16	Dark	320
D	8	White	160
E	8	White	160

Other Units:
   Border: 3" Strips in two colors

   Sewing Instructions: The border is made from 3"-wide strips of two colors.

in color p. 4

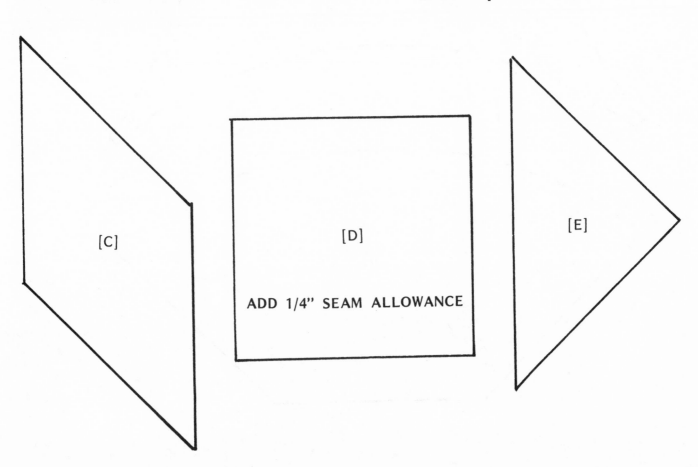

[C]

[D]

ADD 1/4" SEAM ALLOWANCE

[E]

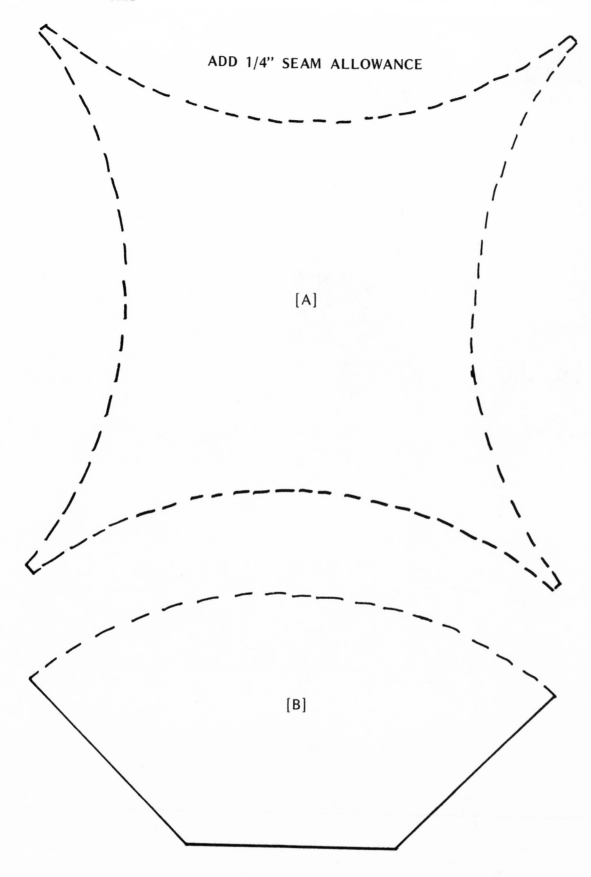

ADD 1/4" SEAM ALLOWANCE

[A]

[B]

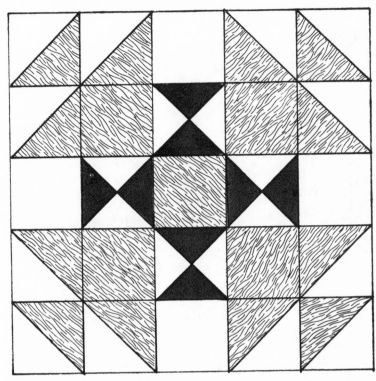

52. Handy Andy

EASY

Quilt Size:	78" x 91"	
Block Size:	13"	
Blocks in Quilt:	42	
	(6 across by 7 down)	

Material:
   5-1/4 yds. Print
   6-1/2 yds. White
   1-1/4 yds. Plain

Pieces per Block			per Quilt
A	4	White	168
	5	Print	210
B	12	Print	504
	12	White	504
C	8	Plain	336
	8	White	336

in color p. 4

Sewing Instructions: Cut out pattern pieces, adding seam allowance, and follow the diagram to piece the block. No border is necessary. This pattern can also be set with lattice strips, or with alternate plain blocks. If lattice strips are used, make a border of the same width as the strips.

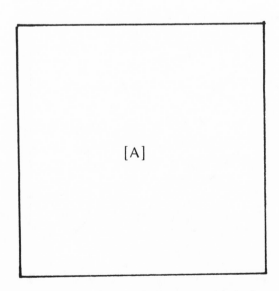

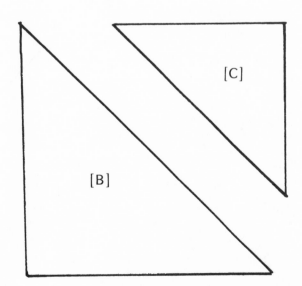

ADD 1/4" SEAM ALLOWANCE

53. Hourglass

EASY

Quilt Size:	81" x 94"
Block Size:	10"
Blocks in Quilt:	42
	(6 across by 7 down)

Material:
   5 yds. White
   2-1/2 yds. Plain (Lattice Strips and Border)
   10" Assorted Prints for each block

Pieces per Block			per Quilt
A	4	White	168
	4	Print	168
B	6	White	252
	6	Print	252

Other Units:
   Lattice Strips
   Border: 3" wide

in color p. 9

Sewing Instructions: Blocks are set together with 3" lattice strips, and top is finished with a 3" border.

ADD 1/4" SEAM ALLOWANCE

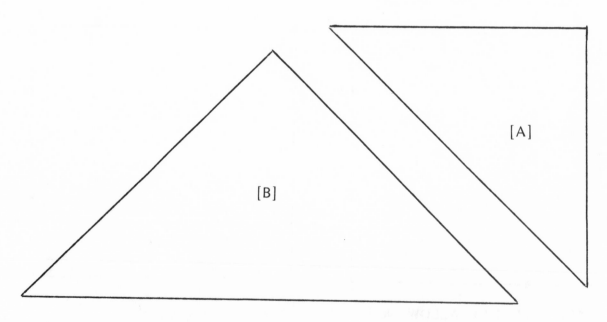

[A]

[B]

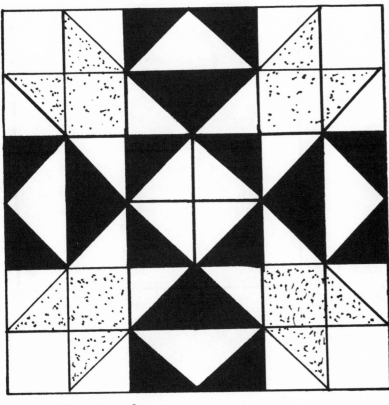

54. Indian Puzzle

MODERATE

Quilt Size:		90" x 108"
Block Size:		18"
Blocks in Quilt:		30
		(5 across by 6 down)

Material:
   7-1/2 yds. White
   3 yds. Blue
   3-3/4 yds. Yellow Print

	Pieces per Block	per Quilt
A	4 White	120
	4 Print	120
B	4 Blue	120
	4 White	120
C	8 Print	240
	12 Blue	360
	20 White	600

in color p. 6

This pattern can be made up in any color combination. The yellow and blue carries out the Indian theme. Other color combinations you might use include brown and yellow, red and yellow, red and green.

   Sewing Instructions: Cut out pattern units, adding 1/4" seam allowance. Assemble the pieces as follows:

Step 1

Assemble 4 per block

Step 2

Assemble 4 per block

Step 3

Assemble 1 per block

Follow the diagram above for color placement.
   When all blocks are completed, set together in strips, 6 blocks across by 7 rows down. Bind the edges with a matching fabric.
   Quilting: Quilt 1/8" from each seam.

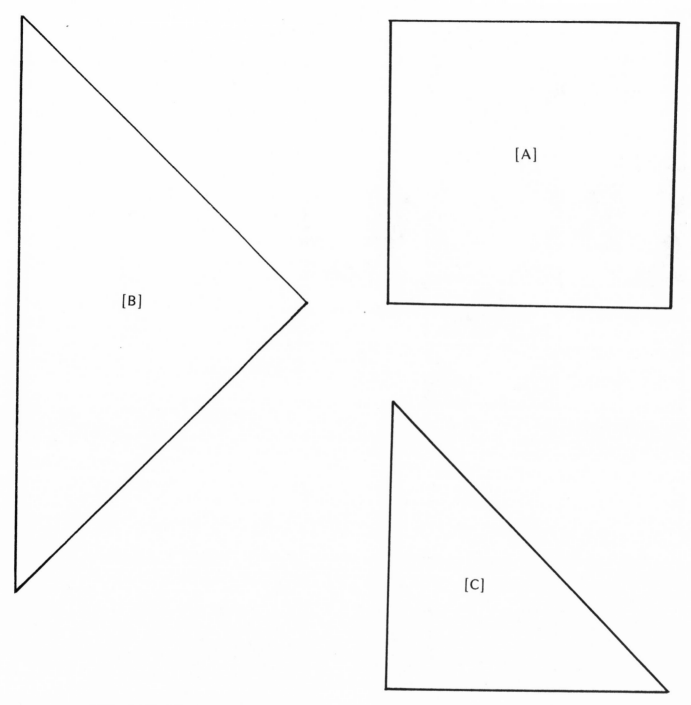

ADD 1/4" SEAM ALLOWANCE

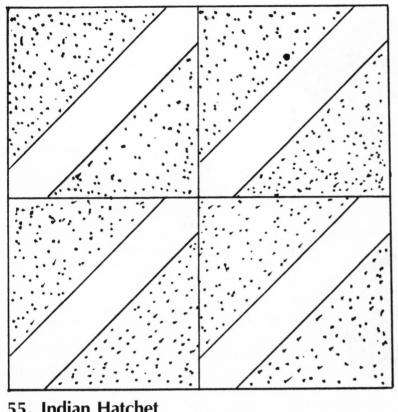

EASY

Quilt Size:	77" x 88"
Block Size:	11"
Blocks in Quilt:	56

(28 pieced, 28 plain, 7 across by 8 down)

Material:

3-1/3 yds. Light Color
3 yds. Dark
2-2/3 yds. Plain (alternate blocks)

Pieces per Block			per Quilt
A	4	Light	112
B	8	Dark	224

in color p. 9

55. Indian Hatchet

[B]

[A]

ADD 1/4" SEAM ALLOWANCE

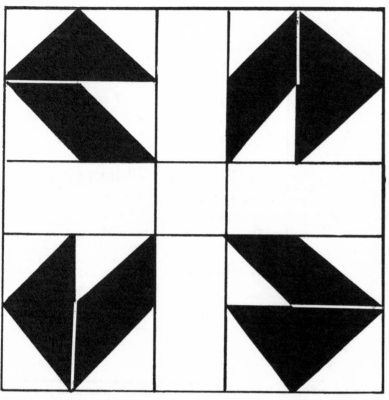

EASY

Quilt Size:	76" x 86"	
Block Size:	10"	
Blocks in Quilt:	56	

(28 pieced, 28 plain; 7 across by 8 down)

Material:
   2-1/2 yds. Red
   6-1/2 yds. White
   2 yds. White

Pieces	per Block		per Quilt
A	1	White	28
B	4	White	112
C	4	Red	112
D	4	Red	112
E	16	White	448

Other Units:
   Border: 3" Red or White Strips

in color p. 5   This pattern is also known as *Whirligig*.

56. Jack in the Box

Sewing Instructions: Cut out pattern pieces, adding 1/4" seam allowance and follow diagram to piece the block.

Border: A 3" wide border of red or white fabric goes around the quilt.

ADD 1/4" SEAM ALLOWANCE

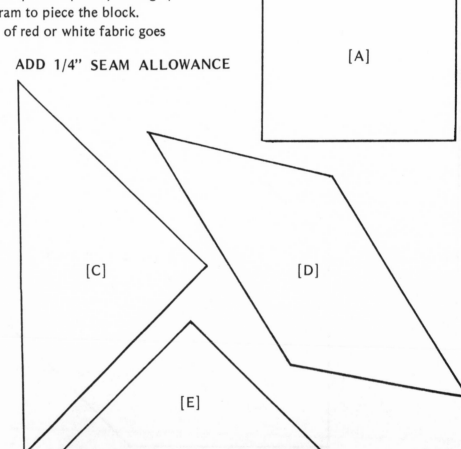

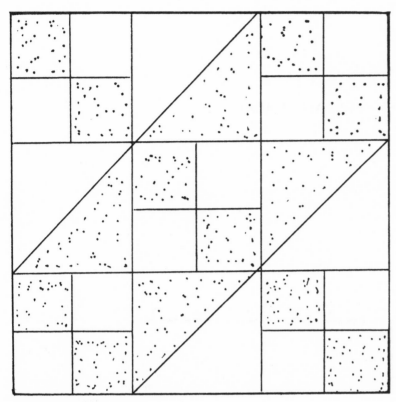

57. Jacob's Ladder

EASY

Quilt Size:	72" x 84"
Block Size:	12"
Blocks in Quilt:	42

   (21 pieced, 21 plain; 6 across by 7 down)

Material:
   2 yds. Color
   7 yds. White

Pieces per Block			per Quilt
A	8	Color	168
	14	White	294
B	4	Color	84
	4	White	84

in color p. 7

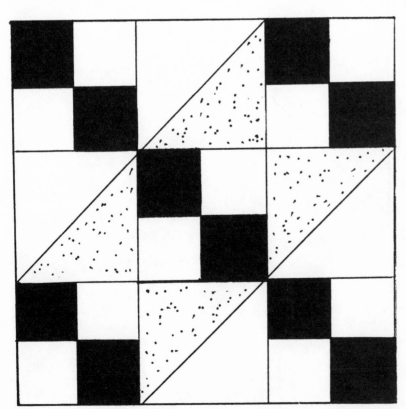

We show two variations for this pattern which dates from the 1700s. In a third variation the ladder goes in the opposite direction.

The names given to this pattern are numerous. The first version is also called *Road to California.* The second version is called *Stepping Stones* in New England and Virginia, *the Tail of Benjamin's Kite* in Pennsylvania, *Trail of the Covered Wagon* or *Wagon Tracks* in the South and Midwest, *the Underground Railroad* in Kentucky, and finally, *Rocky Road to California* or *Rocky Road to Oklahoma.*

Sewing Instructions: A nine patch, the block can be broken into five squares using Piece A, and four squares using Piece B. We have shown yardages for a quilt set with alternate white blocks, but the quilt can be set, and often is, as an allover design. The second version shows the use of a third fabric in the block.

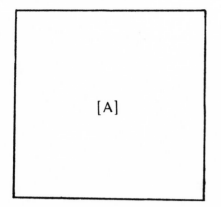

[A]

ADD 1/4" SEAM ALLOWANCE

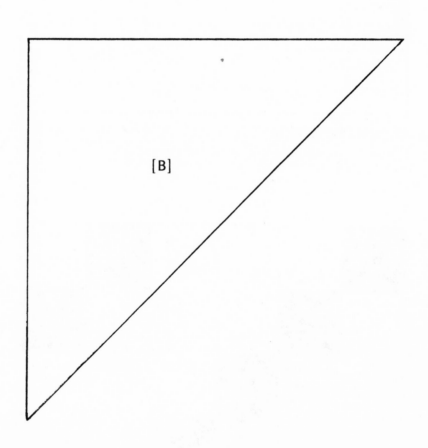

[B]

58. Joseph's Coat

MODERATE

Quilt Size:		75" x 90"
Block Size:		15"
Blocks in Quilt:		30
		(5 across by 6 down)

Material:
   4-1/2 yds. White
   2-1/4 yds. Print
   4 yds. Dark Color

Pieces per Block			**per Quilt**
A	1	Print	30
B	32	White	960
	4	Dark	120
C	4	Dark	120
D	8	Print	240
	8	Dark	240
E	4	Dark	120

in color p. 10

Sewing Instructions: This is assembled as an allover design five rows across and six rows down.

Another version, which is popular in Pennsylvania, joins various colored strips the length of the bed, adding enough strips to fit across. An outside border of the same colors, strips cut about 3" long and stitched together, finish the quilt. Without the border it is known as *Rainbow*.

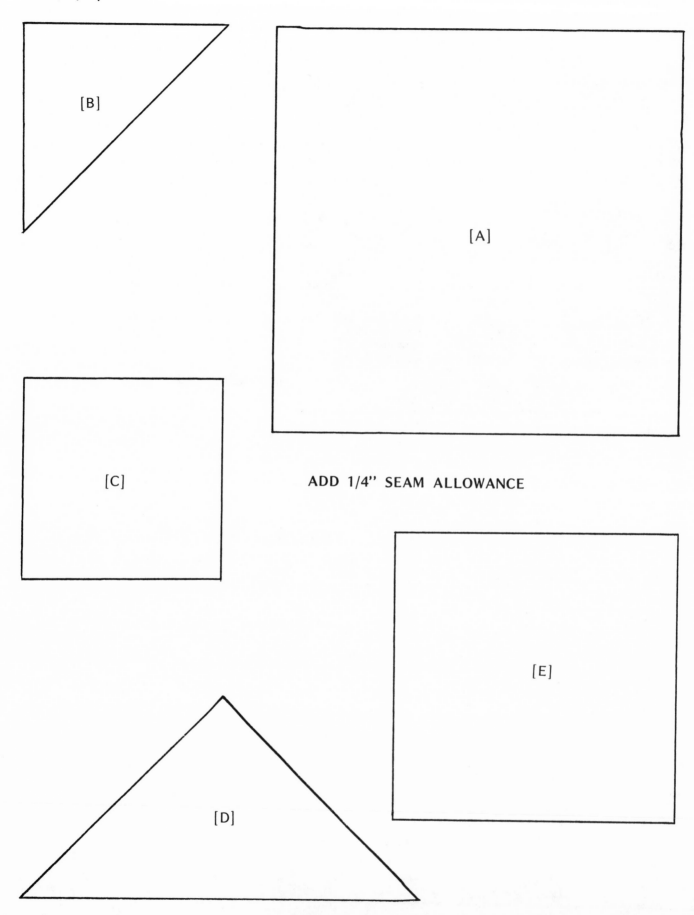

[B]

[A]

[C]

ADD 1/4" SEAM ALLOWANCE

[E]

[D]

59. Kansas Troubles

EASY

Quilt Size:	72" x 90"
Block Size:	18"
Blocks in Quilt:	20
	(4 across by 5 down)

Material:
  7 yds. White
  3-3/4 yds. Color

Pieces per Block			per Quilt
A	4	White	80
B	24	Color	480
	24	White	480
C	4	White	80

in color p. 5

This pattern has at least fourteen different names: *Irish Puzzle, Indian Trails, Forest Path, Rambling Road, North Wind, Winding Walk, Old Maid's Ramble,* and *Storm at Sea* to list a few. From the references to Indians it seems to have originated when the settlers encountered Indians.

  Sewing Instructions: *Kansas Troubles* is usually worked in red and white as an allover design. Some of the other patterns use different color schemes.
  Border: No border is necessary. If desired, a sawtooth border using Piece B would be most appropriate.

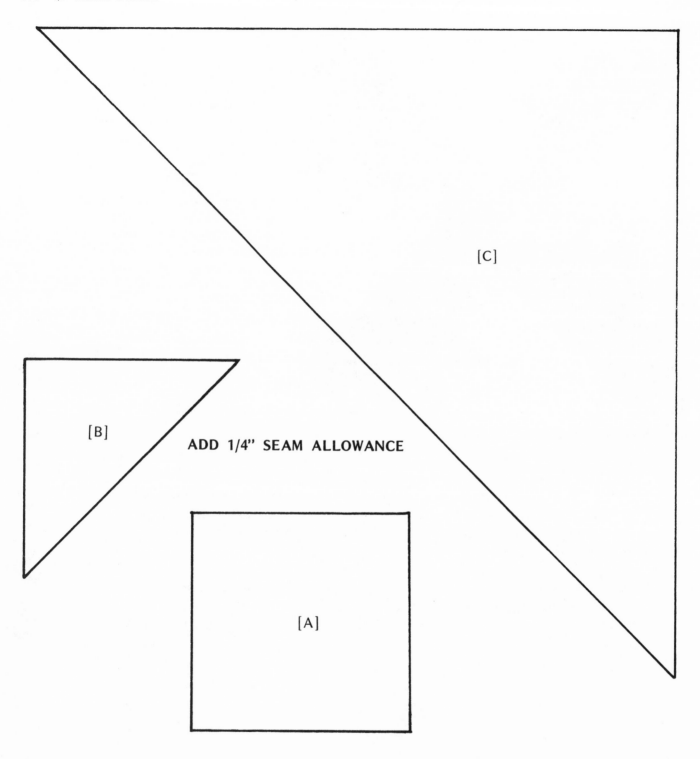

[C]

[B]

ADD 1/4" SEAM ALLOWANCE

[A]

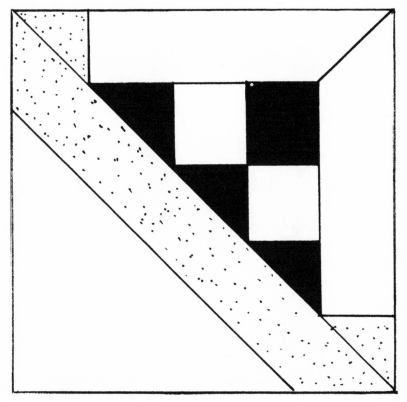

60. King's Crown

EASY

Quilt Size:		76" x 90"	
Block Size:		10"	
Blocks in Quilt:		50	

(30 pieced, 20 plain; 5 across by 6 down)

Material:
6-1/2 yds. White
1-3/4 yds. Gold
1/2 yds. Red

Pieces	per Block		per Quilt
A	1	Gold	30
B	1	White	30
C	2	White	60
D	2	Gold	60
	3	Red	90
E	1	Red	30
	2	White	60

Other Units:
20 Plain Blocks
18 Half Blocks
4 Quarter Blocks
Border: 3" Strips

in color p. 4

This pattern was originated in honor of Napoleon.

Sewing Instructions: The top is set with the blocks running diagonally, alternating with plain white blocks. You will also need the 18 half blocks and 4 quarter blocks to finish the edges.

Another method of setting the top together omits the plain blocks. The top is set in rows and every other block is reversed so that it faces the preceding block.

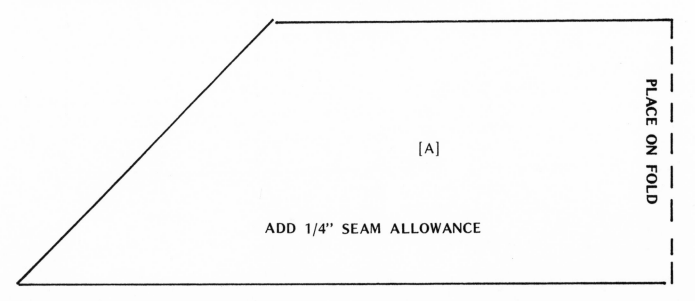

[A]

ADD 1/4" SEAM ALLOWANCE

PLACE ON FOLD

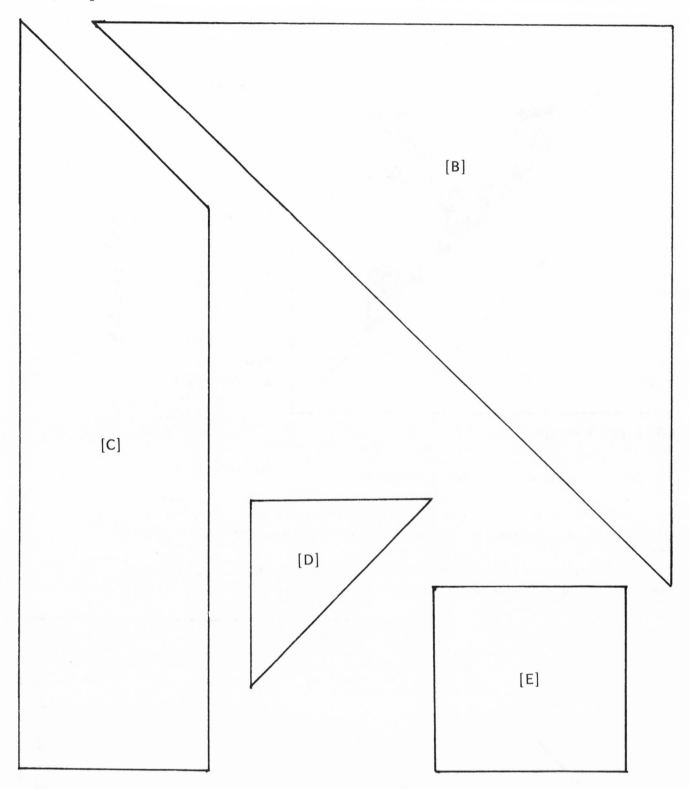

[B]

[C]

[D]

[E]

ADD 1/4" SEAM ALLOWANCE

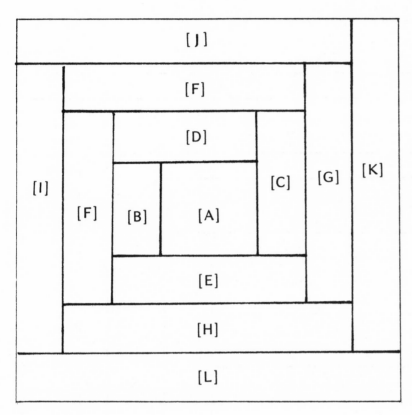

This is probably the most popular quilt pattern ever devised. It is a scrap design. The only rule seems to be that the center square be red.

There are infinite variations in assembling this block, a few of which are illustrated below and on the next page.

In working the pattern, make one side dark and the other side light.

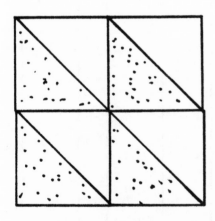

Simple Arrangement

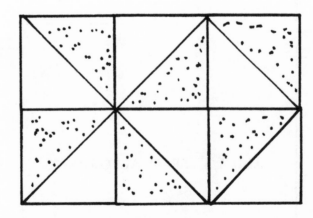

Pinwheel

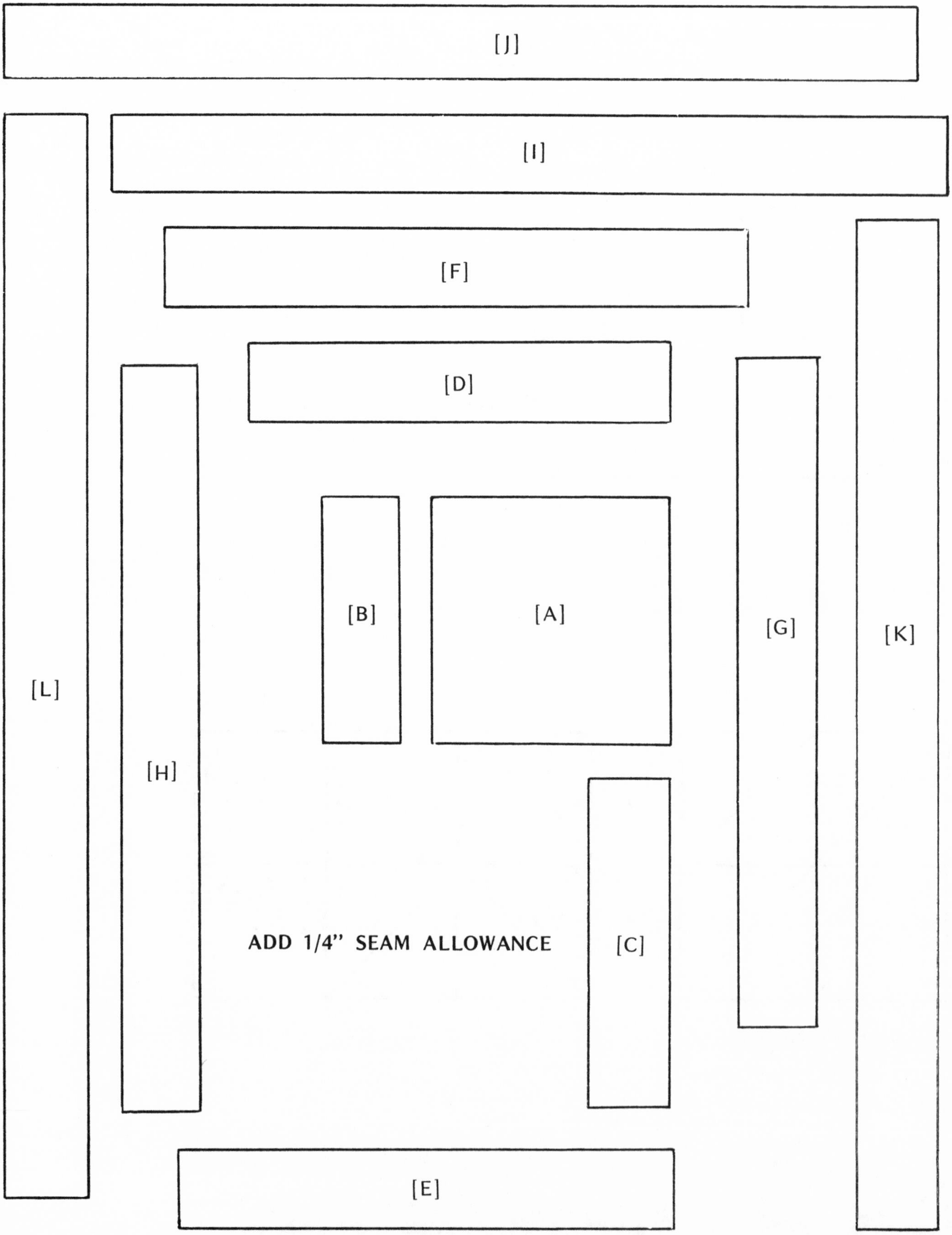

[J]

[I]

[F]

[D]

[L]

[H]

[B]

[A]

[G]

[K]

ADD 1/4" SEAM ALLOWANCE

[C]

[E]

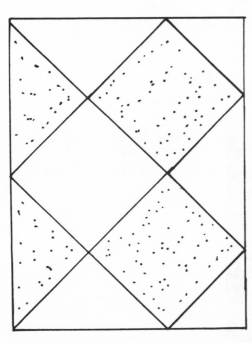

Sunshine and Shadow

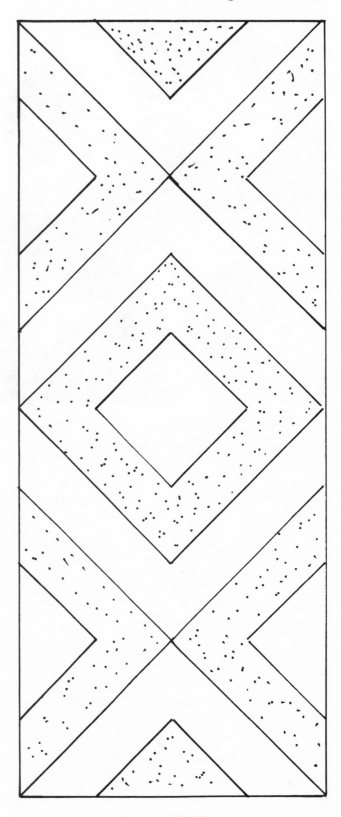

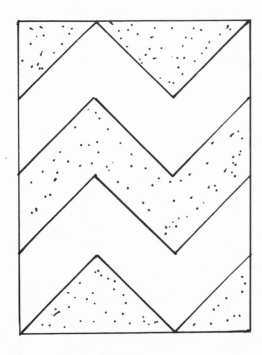

Zig Zag

Square with Ring

62. Kansas Dugout

EASY

Quilt Size:	80" x 80"
Block Size:	10"
Blocks in Quilt:	64
	(8 across by 8 down)

Material:
  4-3/4 yds. White
  4-3/4 yds. Color

	Pieces per Block		**per Quilt**
A	8	Color	512
	8	White	512
B	3	Color	192
	2	White	128

in color p. 12

Sewing Instructions: Cut out pattern pieces, adding seam allowances. Pieces C and D are not used in the blocks, but along the edge of the quilt top to square it. The quilt should be made up as an allover design with no plain blocks or lattice strips.

ADD 1/4" SEAM ALLOWANCE

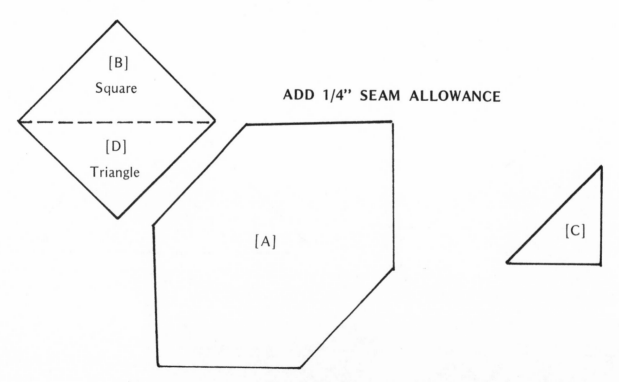

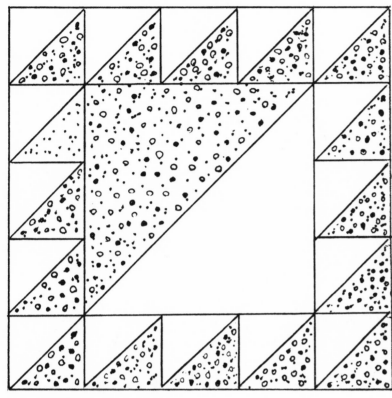

EASY

Quilt Size:	91" x 91"
Block Size:	13"
Blocks in Quilt:	49
	(7 across and 7 down)

Material:
8 yds. Print
2-1/2 yds. Plain
6 yds. White

		Pieces per Block	per Quilt
A	1	Print	49
	1	Plain	49
B	16	Print	784
	16	White	784

in color p. 8

63. Lady of the Lake

A long-time favorite, this pattern originated in Connecticut in 1810 to honor the tales of Sir Walter Scott.

Sewing Instructions: This pattern is set as an allover design. It can also be set diagonally. In the latter case, you will need only 41 pieced blocks, (5 across by 5 down), 16 half blocks, and 4 quarter blocks, for a quilt measuring 90" square. The two settings give totally different looks to the same block.

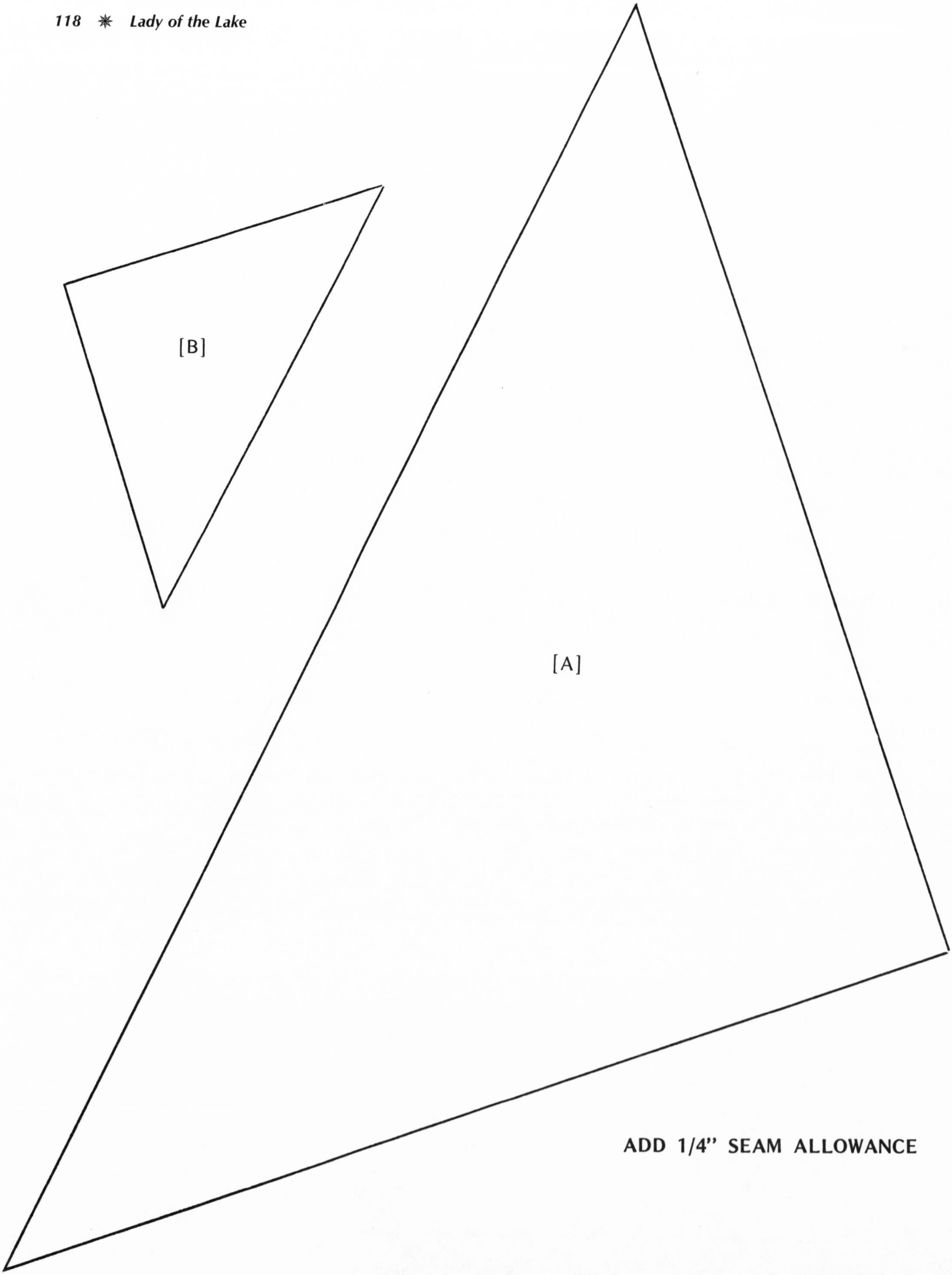

[B]

[A]

ADD 1/4" SEAM ALLOWANCE

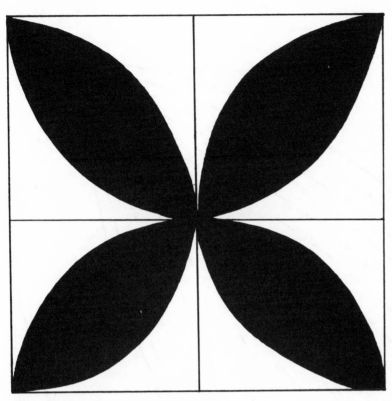

MODERATE

Quilt Size:	90" x 114"
Block Size:	12"
Blocks in Quilt:	48
	(6 across and 8 down)

Material:
 5-1/2 yds. Orange
 7-1/2 yds. White

Pieces per Block		per Quilt
A	4 Orange	192
B	8 White	384

Other Units:
 Border: 2 Orange Strips, 3" wide;
  2 White Strips, 6" wide.

in color p. 2

64. Lafayette Orange Peel

The story behind this pattern says that when General Lafayette visited Philadelphia, a young lady attending a reception in his honor carried off an orange peel from an orange he had eaten. Thus, the quilt is made up traditionally in orange and white. If you like, though, any other color combination can be used.

 Sewing Instructions: Cut out the pattern pieces, allowing 1/4" seam allowance. Stitch a Piece B to each side of Piece A. Make four such units and stitch them together to form the block. When setting the blocks together, take care that the points all meet at the corner exactly so that the pattern is carried from one block to the next for an overall effect.

 Border: Cut two orange strips, 3-1/2" wide by 72" long. Stitch to each 72" end. Cut two orange strips, 3-1/2" wide x 102" long, and stitch to the long sides. Next, cut two strips of white, 6-1/2" wide x 78" long, and stitch to the short sides. Cut 2 strips white, 6-1/2" wide x 108-1/2" long, and stitch to long sides to complete the quilt.

 Quilting: Outline stitch 1/4" from each seam. To fill in on the orange sections, quilt 1/4" apart following the shape of the pattern.

ADD 1/4" SEAM ALLOWANCE

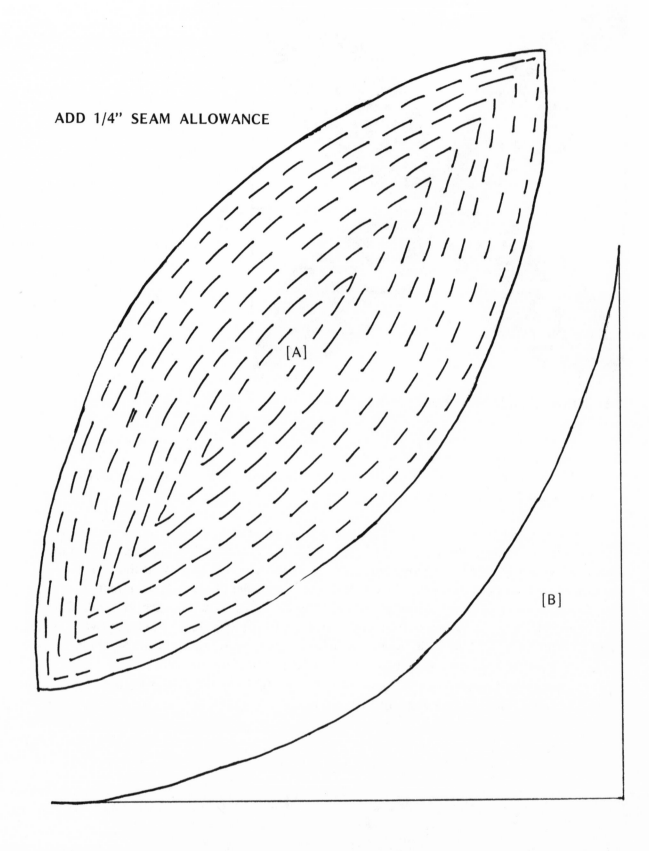

[A]

[B]

65. Lincoln's Platform

EASY

Quilt Size:	70" x 98"
Block Size:	14"
Blocks in Quilt:	35
	(5 across by 7 down)

Material:
  1-3/4 yds. Blue
  1 yd. Red Print
  1-5/8 yds. Blue Print
  3-1/4 yds. White
  2-1/4 yds. Plain Red

Pieces	per Block		per Quilt
A	4	Blue	140
B	4	Red Print	140
C	4	Blue	140
D	4	Blue Print	140
E	8	White	280
	13	Red	455
	4	White	140

in color p. 7

This pattern commemorates the Lincoln-Douglas debates in the 1858 senatorial election.

  Sewing Instructions: Cut out design pieces, adding 1/4" seam allowance. To assemble, stitch Piece A to B to C to D. Make four such units. Outside edge: stitch a red Piece E to a white E to a red E. Make four. Stitch to one side of the previously made units. Now you need a red and white E. Stitch to section as shown in diagram. Join two assembled squares together with Piece F between them. Join two Pieces F to a red Piece E. Stitch this unit to the bottom of the rectangle. Assemble the bottom two squares in the same manner.
  Border: This quilt pattern forms its own border.
  Quilting: Quilt 1/4" on each side of all seams. The long Piece F portions can be quilted with a small cable stitch or with diamonds.

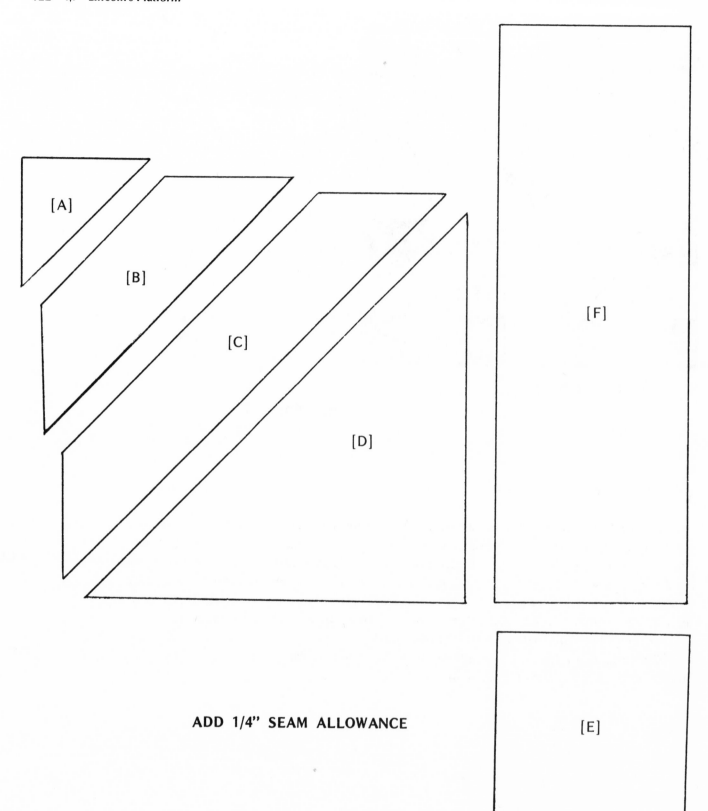

[A]

[B]

[C]

[D]

[F]

ADD 1/4" SEAM ALLOWANCE

[E]

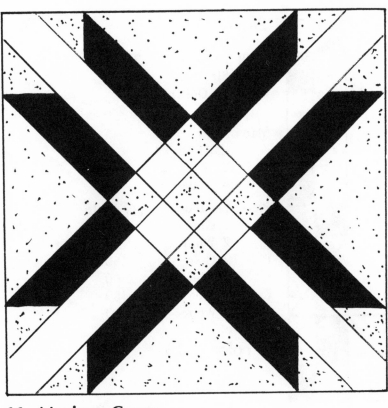

MODERATE

Quilt Size:		74" x 84"
Block Size:		10-1/2"
Blocks in Quilt:		56
		(7 across by 8 down)

Material:
   3-1/4 yds. White
   2 yds. Red Print
   4-3/4 yds. Yellow Print

Pieces	per Block		per Quilt
A	4	White	224
	5	Yellow	
		Print	280
B	4	White	224
C	8	Red Print	448
D	8	Yellow	
		Print	448
E	4	Yellow	
		Print	224

in color p. 4

66. Mexican Cross

This pattern is also called *Mexican Star* and *Star and Cross.*

Sewing Instructions: This is a rather slow pattern to put together, but the results are well worth it. Blocks are set in rows 7 across and 8 down. The diagonal strips form an all-over pattern when completed.

[E]

ADD 1/4" SEAM ALLOWANCE

[C]

[D]

[B]

[A]

124 ✳ Milky Way

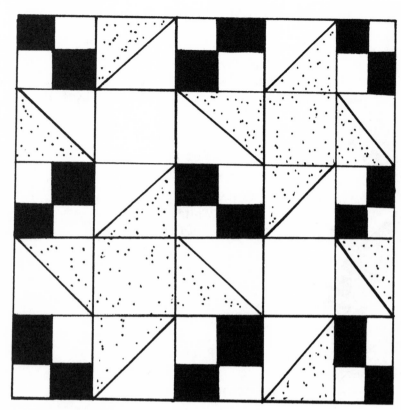

67. Milky Way

EASY

Quilt Size:	75" x 90"	
Block Size:	15"	
Blocks in Quilt:	30	
	(5 across by 6 down)	

Material:
- 4 yds. Gold
- 5 yds. White
- 2 yds. Blue

	Pieces per Block		per Quilt
A	2	Gold	60
	2	White	60
B	12	Gold	360
	12	White	360
C	18	Blue	480
	18	White	480

in color p. 10

Sewing Instructions: Cut out pattern pieces, adding seam allowances. Set blocks flush for an allover design. Alternatively, you can piece four blocks for the center and surround them with border strips of the three colors to fit the size of the bed.

ADD 1/4" SEAM ALLOWANCE

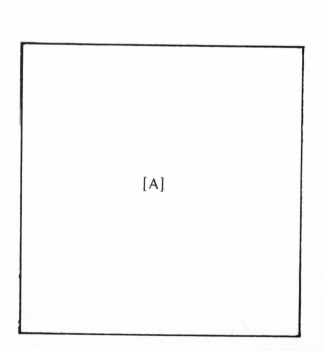

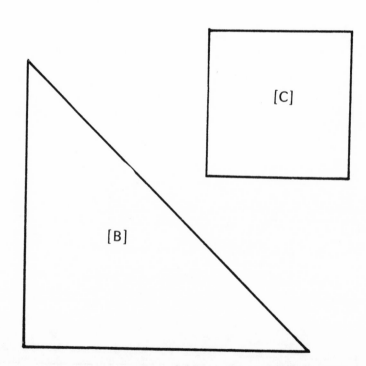

68. Monkey Wrench

EASY

Quilt Size:	78" x 88"
Block Size:	10"
Blocks in Quilt:	78

(28 pieced, 28 plain; 7 across by 8 down)

Material:
4-1/2 yds. White
4-1/2 yds. Color

Pieces per Block			per Quilt
A	2	Color	56
	2	White	56
B	2	Color	56
	2	White	56
C	2	White	56
	2	Color	56
D	2	Color	56
	2	White	56

Other Units:
12 White Squares, 10"
16 Dark Squares, 10"

in color p. 8

This pattern is also called *Snail's Trail*. In pioneer days in Indiana, this was called *Indiana Puzzle*.

Sewing Instructions: Piece twenty-eight blocks as shown in the diagram. The rows are set with alternate dark and light plain blocks. Below is the setting design. P indicates pieced block, W indicates white plain block and D indicates color plain block.

```
P   W   P   W   P   W   P
D   P   D   P   D   P   D
P   W   P   W   P   W   P
D   P   D   P   D   P   D
P   W   P   W   P   W   P
D   P   D   P   D   P   D
P   W   P   W   P   W   P
D   P   D   P   D   P   D
```

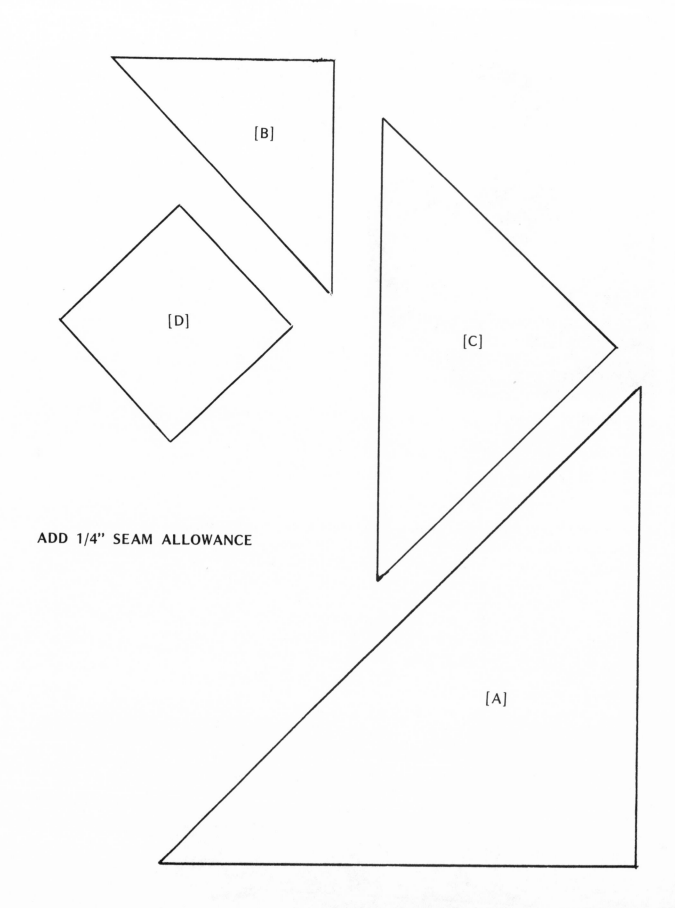

ADD 1/4" SEAM ALLOWANCE

69. Mohawk Trail

MODERATE

Quilt Size:	78" x 97"
Block Size:	17"
Blocks in Quilt:	20
	(4 across by 5 down)

Material:
    5 yds. White (background)
    2 yds. Dark Harmonizing Fabric
            (lattice strips)
    Assorted Scraps (design units)

Pieces per Block
A   48 Assorted Prints and Plains
1 Background Block, 18" square

Other Units:
28   Lattice Strips, 3" x 18"

in color p. 15

This makes up into a very pretty scrap quilt. The dark lattice strips help to tie the whole quilt together. It is a very old pattern, which, from the name, probably dates from early frontier days.

   Sewing Instructions: Cut out the design pieces, allowing 1/4" seam allowance. Cut out twenty background blocks, 18" square. (This allows a 1/2" seam allowance.) Cut out twenty-eight lattice strips, 3" x 18" (includes seam allowance).
   Stitch together 8 units using 3 design pieces, and 4 units using 6 design pieces. Following the diagram, place these assembled units on the block, pinning or basting them in place to be sure they are properly aligned before final stitching. When everything is properly arranged, stitch in place with small hemming stitches.
   Setting the Blocks: Add a lattice strip to bottom and side of first three blocks in a row and to the bottom of the final block in the row. Join the blocks together. Continue in this manner until the quilt is complete. Add a 2" border to outside edges.

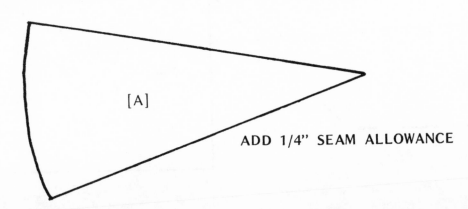

[A]

ADD 1/4" SEAM ALLOWANCE

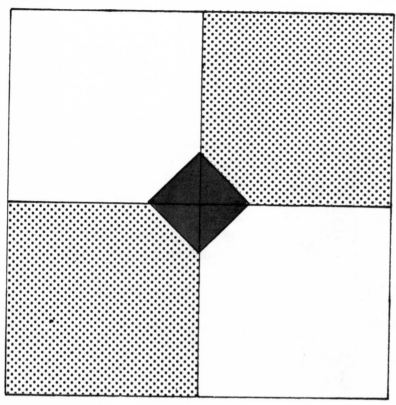

EASY

Quilt Size:	80-1/2" x 97-1/2"
Block Size:	8-1/2"
Blocks in Quilt:	99

(45 pieced, 44 plain; 9 across by 11 down)

Material:
4-1/2 yds. White
Scraps (tie)

Pieces per Block			per Quilt
A	2	White	90
	2	Scrap	90
B	1	Scrap Plain	45

Other Units:
44 Plain Blocks, 9" square
Border: 2 Strips, 2-1/2" x 87";
2 Strips, 2-1/2" x 99"

in color p. 6

70. Necktie

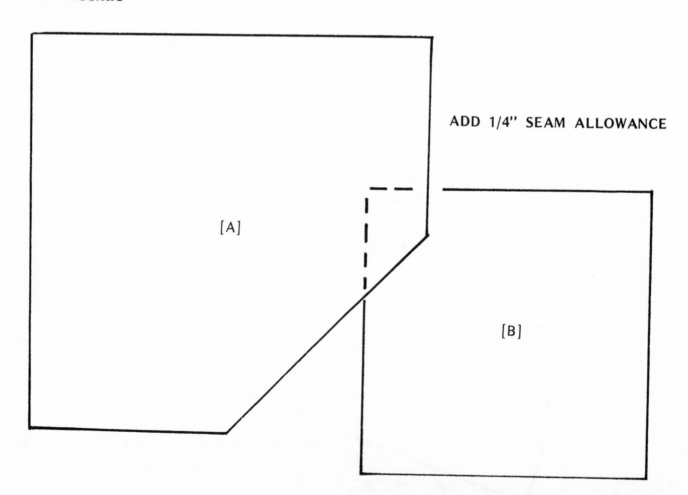

ADD 1/4" SEAM ALLOWANCE

[A]

[B]

71. North Carolina Lily

MODERATE

Quilt Size:	85" x 102"	
Block Size:	12"	
Blocks in Quilt:	50	

(30 pieced, 20 plain; 5 across by 6 down)

Material:
 1-3/4 yds. Yellow Print
 7-3/4 yds. White
 2 yds. Dark Green

Pieces	per Block		per Quilt
A	12	Print	360
B	6	White	180
C	3	White	90
D	3	Green	90
E	2	White	60
F	1	White	30
G	2	Green	60
H	1	Green	30

Other Units:
20 Plain Blocks, 12-1/2" square
18 Half Blocks
 4 Quarter Blocks

in color p. 11

This pattern underwent several name changes as it traveled across the country. In Tennessee and Kentucky it was called *Mountain Lily;* in Ohio and Illinois, *Fire Lily;* in New England, *Wood Lily;* in the Middle West, *Prairie Lily* or *Noonday Lily;* in Connecticut, *Meadow Lily;* and in California, *Mariposa Lily.*

 Sewing Instructions: To assemble this quilt, set the top with the blocks on the diagonal, alternating plain and pieced blocks. You will need 20 blocks, 12-1/2" square, 18 half blocks and 4 quarter blocks. The stems (patterns not given) are cut on the bias about 1/2" wide. For a quilt of this size, binding off the edges should suffice. If you prefer a border, make the quilt smaller by one row in each direction, and cut the border to make up the difference. The lily pattern can be appliqued to the border.

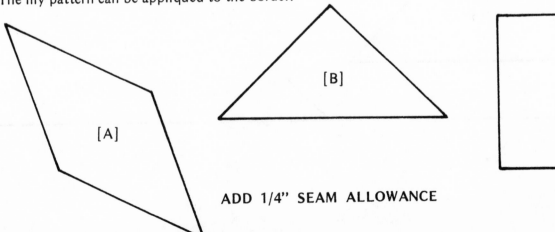

[A]

[B]

[C]

ADD 1/4" SEAM ALLOWANCE

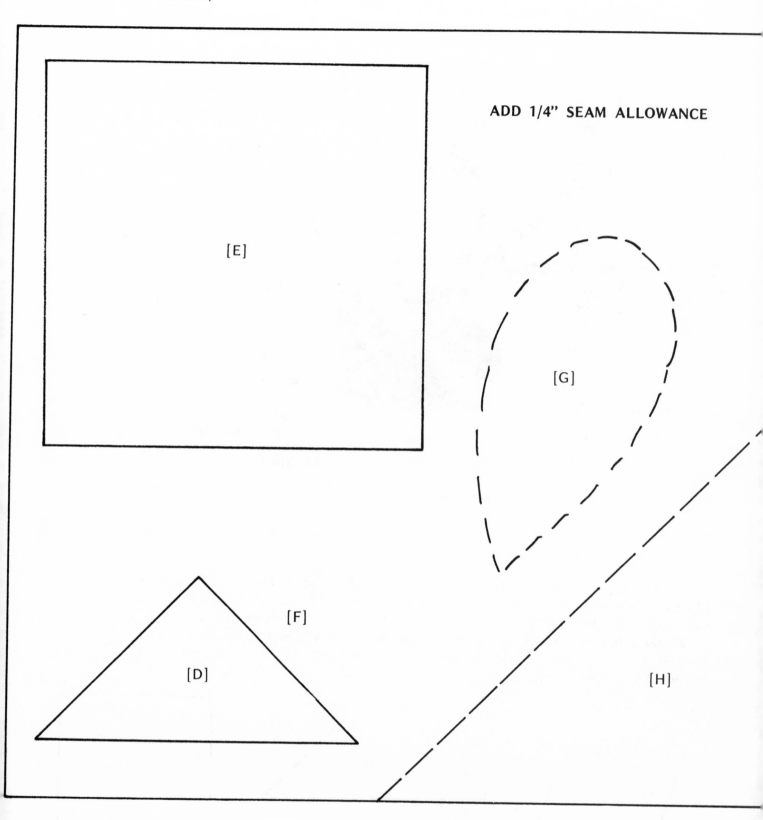

ADD 1/4" SEAM ALLOWANCE

[E]

[G]

[F]

[D]

[H]

72. Ocean Wave II

EASY

Quilt Size:	85" x 102"
Block Size:	17"
Blocks in Quilt:	30
	(5 across by 6 down)

Material:
  8 yds. White
  4-1/3 yds. Color

Pieces per Block			per Quilt
A	1	White	30
B	48	White	1440
	48	Color	1440
C	4	White	120

in color p. 8

This pattern dates from at least the 1880s. The Amish used bright, jewel-like colors in making this quilt. Robert Bishop, in *New Discoveries in American Quilts*, shows a color plate of this pattern using black or navy blue for the center and corner pieces, and shades of orange, red, blue, and green for all of the triangles. There is no white.

   Sewing Instructions: Cut out pattern pieces, adding 1/4" seam allowance. Following the diagram above, divide the block into four parts. Piece each quarter of the small triangles, and add the corner block. Stitch this to the center block. Continue until the block is finished.
   Quilting: Quilt around each pattern unit 1/8" from seam. A floral motif may be used for the center square.

ADD 1/4" SEAM ALLOWANCE

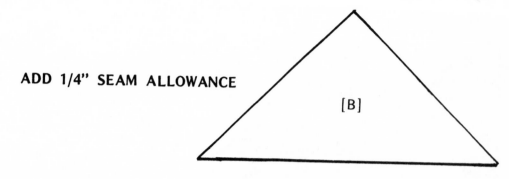

[B]

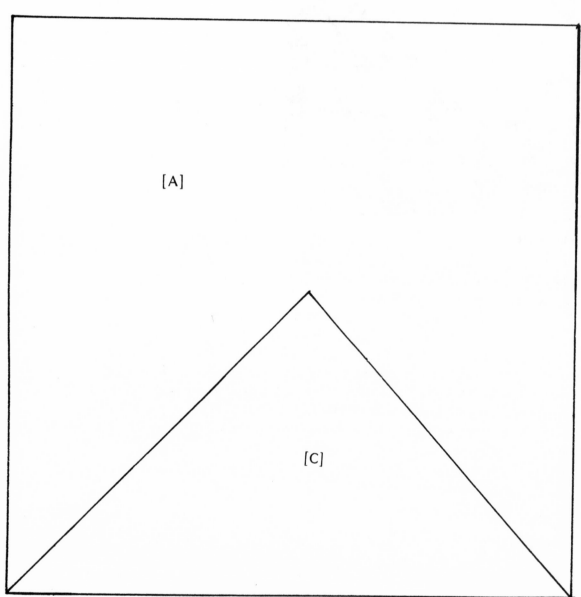

[A]

[C]

73. Odd Fellows' Chain

EASY

Quilt Size:	72" x 84"
Block Size:	12"
Blocks in Quilt:	42
	(6 across by 7 down)

Material:
  5 yds. Color
  6-1/2 yds. White

Pieces per Block			per Quilt
A	1	White	42
B	12	White	504
C	24	Color	1008
	40	White	1680
D	8	Color	336

in color p. 5

This seems to be an old pattern although no precise date is available. The favored colors are red and white or yellow and white.

Sewing Instructions: This is really a simple pattern to assemble, in spite of its many parts. It will be simpler if you break the pattern down into four smaller blocks and assemble these, then join them to the center square. To form into units: Join two Pieces C, one white and one color, to form a square. (You will need two for each corner.) Join two of these to two Piece B to form the corner. Assemble a square from one color and one white Piece C, add a white C to each side. Join this to a D. Attach this to the previous unit. Continue, following the diagram; then join all the completed units to the center square, Piece A. No border is required.

Quilting: Quilt 1/8" from all seams.

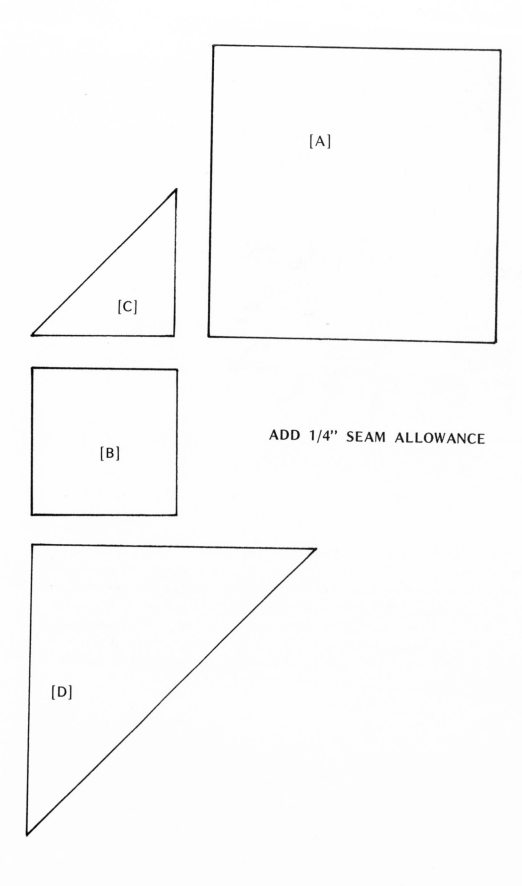

[A]

[C]

[B]

ADD 1/4" SEAM ALLOWANCE

[D]

74. Our Village Green

EASY

Quilt Size:	72" x 84"	
Block Size:	12"	
Blocks in Quilt:	42	
	(6 across by 7 down)	

Material:
5-1/2 yds. Green Print or Plain
7 yds. White

Pieces per Block			per Quilt
A	24	Green Print or Plain	1008
B	1	White	1008

in color p. 12

This pattern title recalls memories of our early heritage, of small, quiet villages and meetings and band concerts on the Village Green.

Sewing Instructions: Cut out pattern parts, allowing 1/4" seam allowance. Piece alternate green and white Piece A to form strips as shown in the diagram. The outer row consists of four triangles across, the inner three. Seam these together in rows. Then stitch them to the center piece to complete the block. Stitch the blocks together in rows, 6 rows across and 7 rows down.

Border: This quilt can be bound, or a strip border can be applied. We recommend a narrow white strip, then a green strip, and finally a wider white strip. Because this will make the quilt larger, additional material will be required.

Quilting: Simply outline quilt around each unit. The center block allows for a more elaborate motif, such as a floral design.

ADD 1/4" SEAM ALLOWANCE

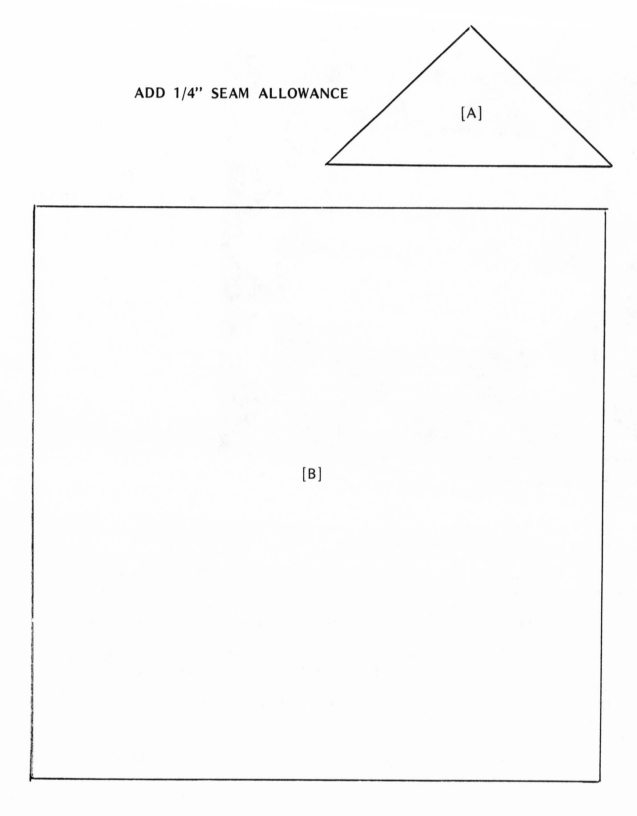

[A]

[B]

EASY

Quilt Size:	84" x 100"
Block Size:	12"
Blocks in Quilt:	30
	(5 across by 6 down)

Material:
- 4-1/2 yds. White
- 2 yds. Color (Lattice Strips and Border)
- 1/2 yd. Assorted Prints

Pieces	per Block	per Quilt
A	2 Print	60
B	4 White	120
C	6 Print	180
	10 White	300

Other Units:
- Lattice Strips, 4" wide
- Border, 4"-6" wide

in color p. 10

75. Old Maid's Puzzle

This excellent scrap quilt dates to at least 1800. Use the same print for each block, and tie it all together with a harmonious color for the lattice strips.

Sewing Instructions: Cut out pattern pieces for each block, adding 1/4" seam allowance. To assemble:

Step 1

Step 2: Make two and stitch together to form upper left and lower right corners.

Step 3

Step 4: Make two such units to form upper right and lower left corners.

  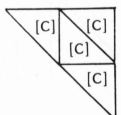 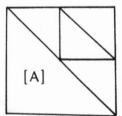

Assemble the completed units into a block as illustrated above. When all the blocks are complete, set them together with 4" lattice strips between the blocks.

Border: Stitch a 4" or 6" strip of the same fabric used for lattice strips around outside edges.

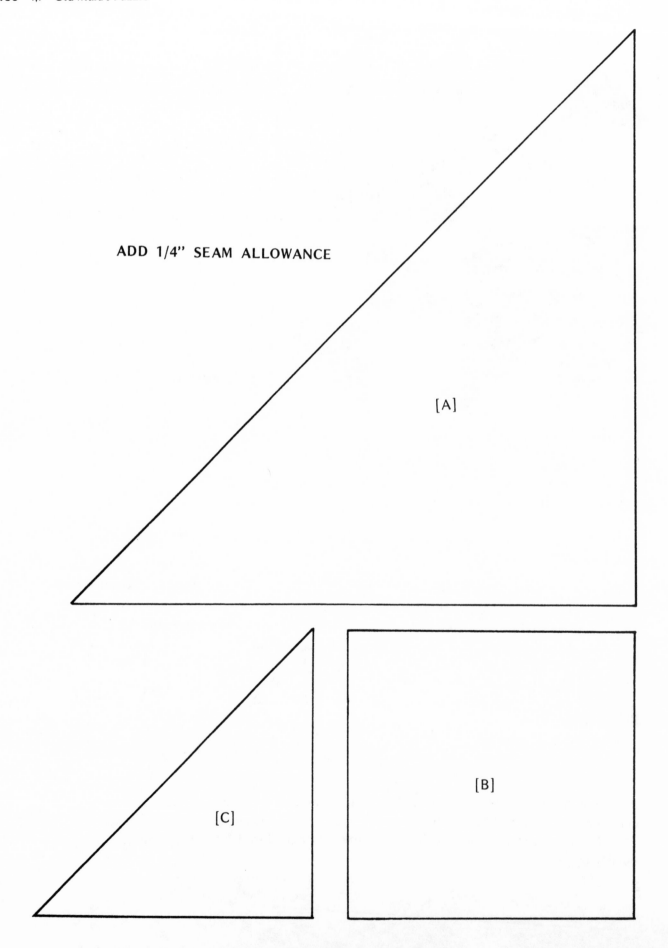

ADD 1/4" SEAM ALLOWANCE

[A]

[C]

[B]

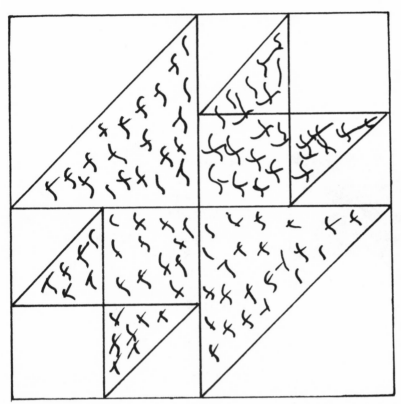

76. Anvil

EASY

Quilt Size:	78" x 93"	
Block Size:	12"	
Blocks in Quilt:	30	
	(5 across by 6 down)	

Material:
   3-3/4 yds. White
   1/4 yd. Assorted Prints
   3 yds. Color (Lattice Strips and Border)

Pieces per Block			per Quilt
A	2	White	60
	2	Print	60
B	2	White	60
	2	Print	60
C	4	White	120
	4	Print	120

Other Units:
58   Lattice Strips, 3-1/2" x 12-1/2"
     Border: 2 Strips, 3-1/2" x 72-1/2";
        2 Strips, 3-1/2" x 93-1/2"

in color p. 8

Anvil and *Crosses and Losses* are made using the same pattern pieces as *Old Maid's Puzzle*, but different fabrics and patterns in the block. *Crosses and Losses* (known also as *Fox and Geese, Double X,* and *X*) can also be set with lattice strips or alternated with plain blocks. The yardage required will have to be adjusted.

77. Crosses & Losses

EASY

Quilt Size:	72" x 84"	
Block Size:	12"	
Blocks in Quilt:	42	
	(6 across by 7 down)	

Material:
   5-1/2 yds. White
   4-1/4 yds. Color

Pieces per Block			per Quilt
A	2	White	84
	2	Color	84
B	4	Color	168
	4	White	168
C	4	White	168

in color p. 6

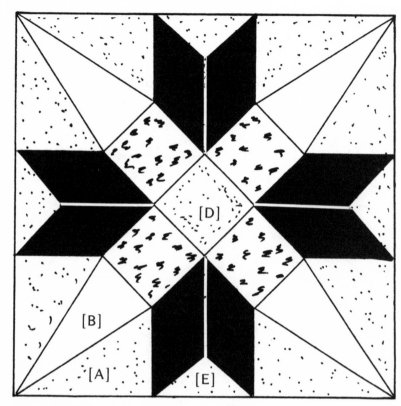

MODERATE

Quilt Size:	70" x 90"
Block Size:	10"
Blocks in Quilt:	63
	(7 across by 9 down)

Material:
  1-1/2 yds. Dark Green
  1 yd. White
  1-1/2 yds. Light Green
  1 yd. Dark Print
  1/4 yd. Light Print

Pieces	per Block		per Quilt
A	8	Dark Green	504
B	4	White	252
C	8	Light Green	504
D	4	Dark Print	252
	1	Light Print	63
E	4	Dark Green	252

in color p. 13

78. Prairie Queen

This pattern appeared in *Household Magazine* in 1937.

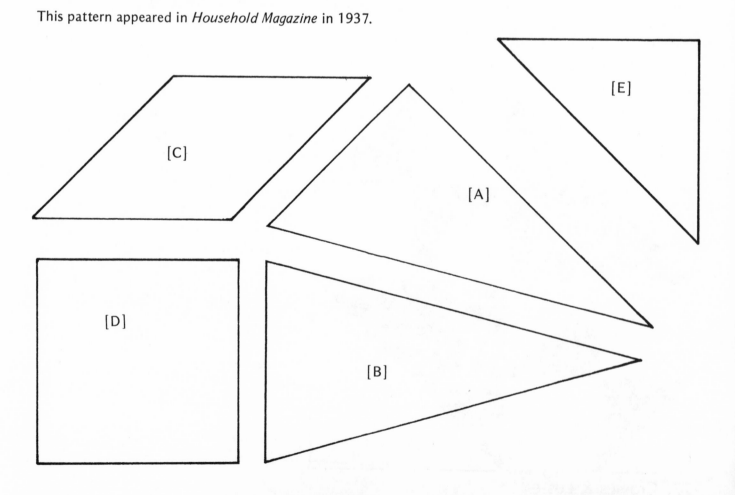

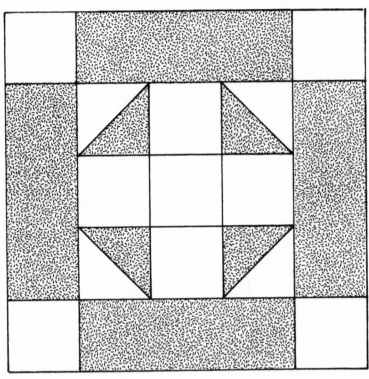

EASY

Quilt Size:	72" x 84"
Block Size:	12"
Blocks in Quilt:	42
	(6 across by 7 down)

Material:
4-1/4 yds. White
4 yds. Print

Pieces	per Block		per Quilt
A	5	White	210
B	4	Print	168
	4	White	168
C	4	Print	168
D	4	White	168

in color p. 12

79. Philadelphia Pavement

This pattern is an old favorite from Pennsylvania.

ADD 1/4" SEAM ALLOWANCE

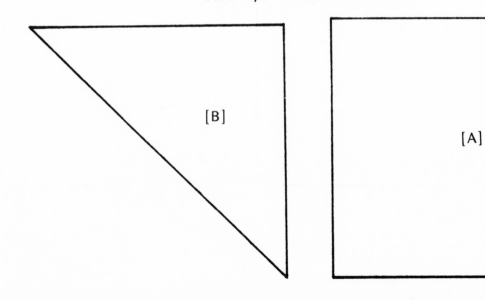

[B]

[A]

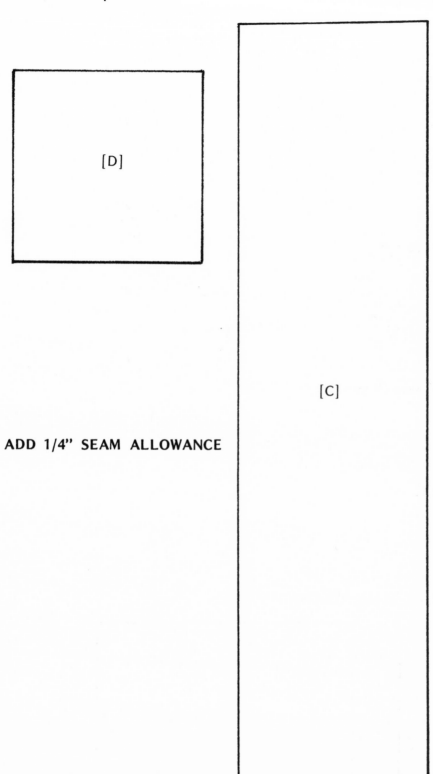

[D]

[C]

ADD 1/4" SEAM ALLOWANCE

80. Pine Tree

EASY

Quilt Size:	75" x 90"
Block Size:	15"
Blocks in Quilt:	30
	(5 across by 6 down)

Material:
   6-1/2 yds. White
   4-1/2 yds. Green

Pieces per Block			per Quilt
A	2	White	60
B	1	Green	30
C	2	Green	60
	3	White	90
D	42	Green	1260
	42	White	1260
E	2	Green	60

in color p. 12

ADD 1/4" SEAM ALLOWANCE

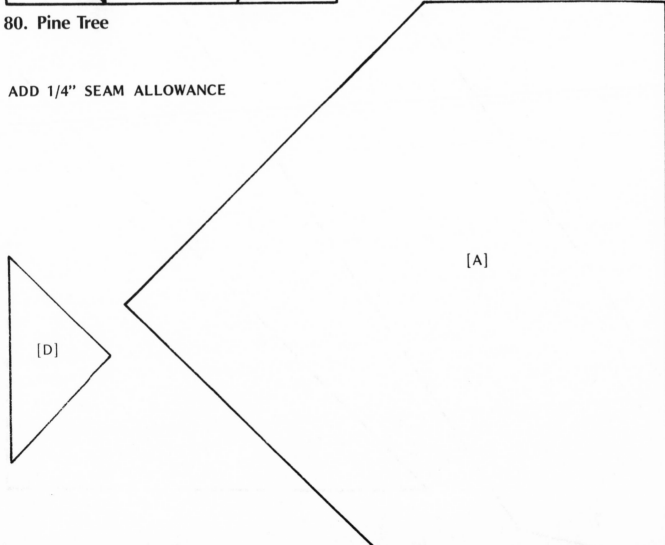

[A]

[D]

[E]

ADD 1/4" SEAM ALLOWANCE

[B]

[C]

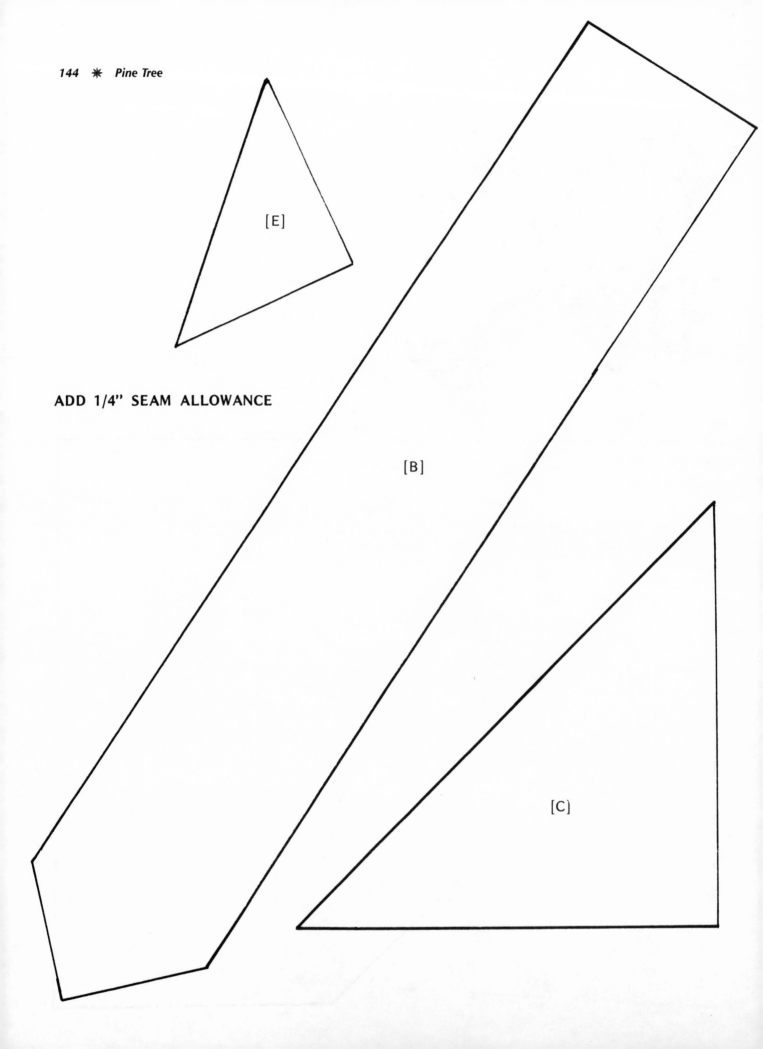

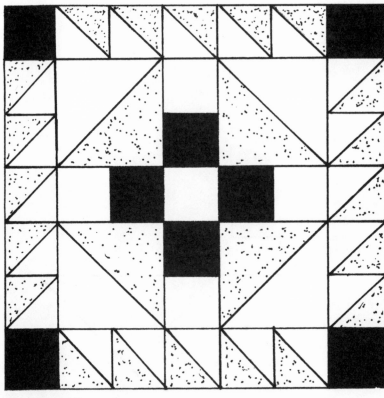

EASY

Quilt Size:	70" x 84"	
Block Size:	14"	
Blocks in Quilt:	30	
	(5 across by 6 down)	

Material:
  1-1/2 yds. Dark
  5-1/4 yds. Soft Lime Green
  4-1/2 yds. Green and Yellow Print

Pieces per Block			per Quilt
A	8	Dark	240
	5	Green	150
B	20	Green	600
	20	Print	600
C	4	Green	120
	4	Print	120

in color p. 12

81. Prickly Pear

This pattern dates from the late 1700s or early 1800s.

Sewing Instructions: Cut out pattern units, adding 1/4" seam allowance. To assemble: Break the block down into four smaller blocks, with the center strips to be added last. For each corner block you will need to assemble four Piece B, one green and one print triangle, and one Piece C, one green and one print. When assembled, join as shown in diagram. To join center strips, make four Piece B, of one green and one print triangle; stitch to a green square and then a brown square.

Border: No border is necessary, but one may be added if you desire. You may also join the blocks together with lattice strips rather than side by side.

Quilting: Quilt 1/8" from all seams.

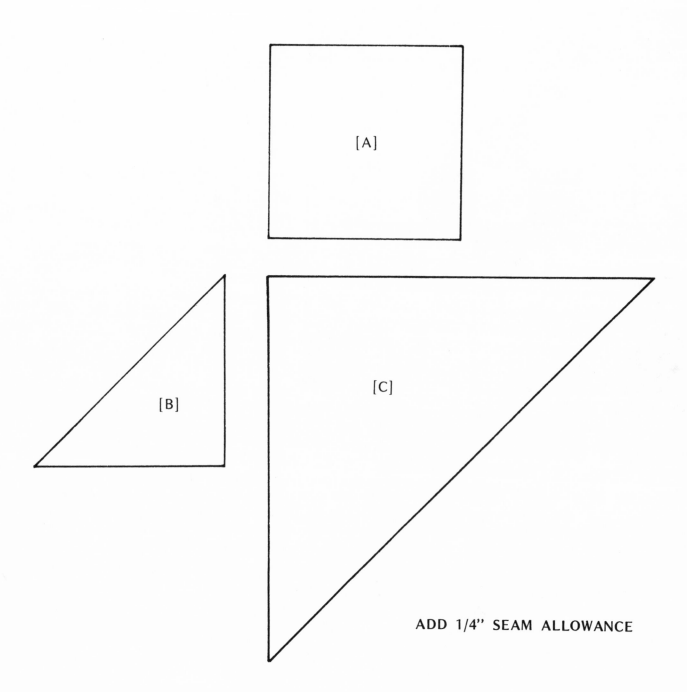

ADD 1/4" SEAM ALLOWANCE

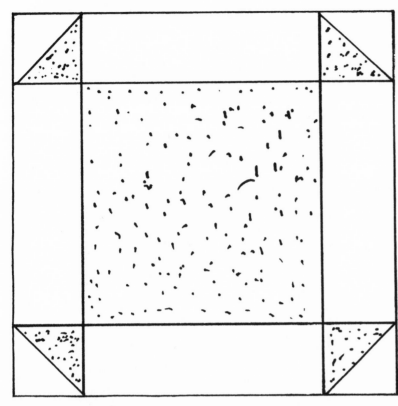

EASY

Quilt Size:	81" x 90"
Block Size:	9"
Blocks in Quilt:	90
	(9 across by 10 down)

Material:
4-1/3 yds. White
3 yds. Print

Pieces per Block			per Quilt
A	4	White	360
	4	Print	360
B	4	White	360
C	1	Print	90

in color p. 4

82. Puss in the Corner

This is one of those patterns with several versions: *Kitty Corner* and *Tic Tac Toe* are other names. This one dates from about 1800. Other patterns known as *Puss in the Corner* are *Aunt Sukey's Choice, Churn Dash* and *Golden Gate.*

    Sewing Instructions: Cut out pattern pieces, adding 1/4" seam allowance, and put together following the diagram.

ADD 1/4" SEAM ALLOWANCE

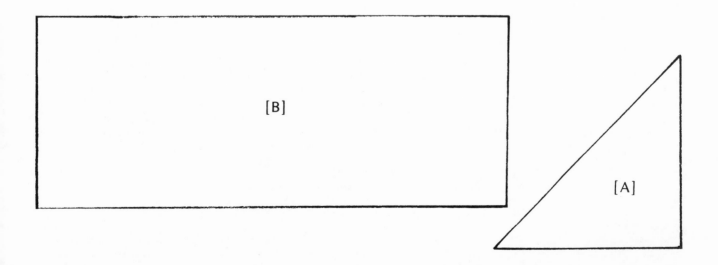

[B]

[A]

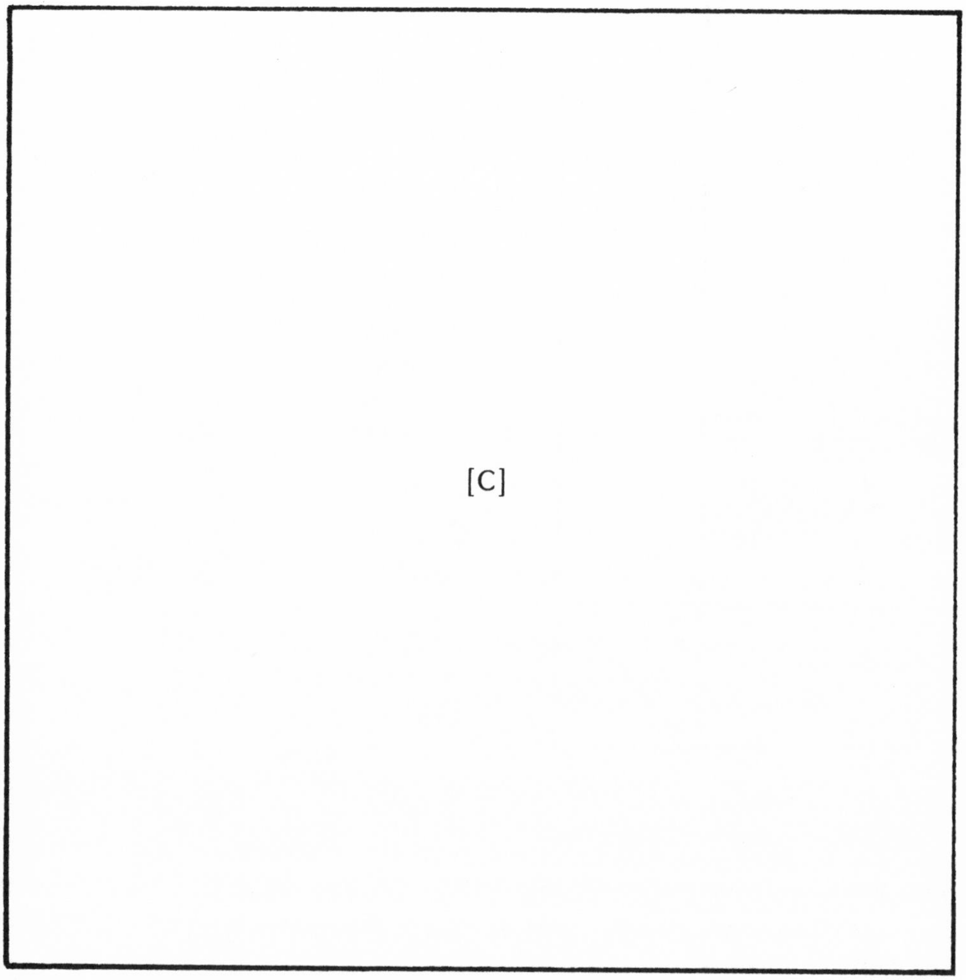

[C]

ADD 1/4" SEAM ALLOWANCE

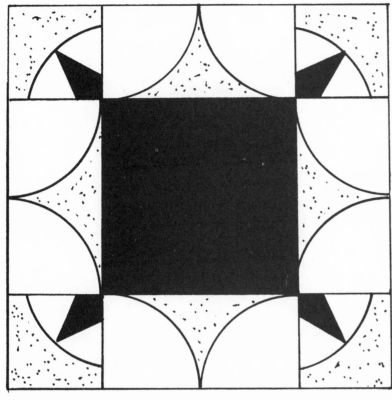

DIFFICULT

Quilt Size:	72" x 96"	
Block Size:	12"	
Blocks in Quilt:	48	
	(6 across by 8 down)	

Material:
   3-1/2 yds. Color
   5 yds. Print
   7 yds. White

Pieces	per Block		per Quilt
A	1	Color	48
B	8	White	384
C	8	White	384
D	4	Color	192
E	4	Print	192
F	4	Print	192

in color p. 7

83. Queen's Pride

Sewing Instructions: Break the pattern into four corner units and four center units, and assemble each of these. When completed, join them around the center square.

This quilt may be done as an allover design or as a scrap pattern. If you choose to do it as a scrap pattern, join the blocks with lattice strips in a harmonizing color. Changes will have to be made in the size of the quilt.

Border: If an allover pattern, no border is necessary. If you have joined the blocks with lattice strips, add a border strip of the same width to the outside edges.

Quilting: Quilt 1/8" from all seams.

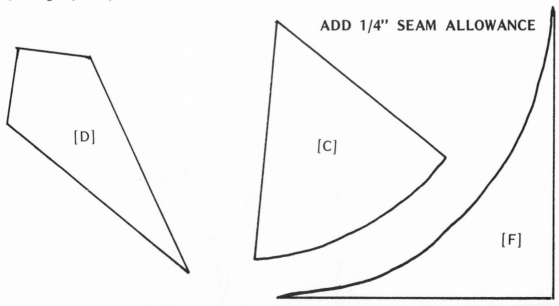

ADD 1/4" SEAM ALLOWANCE

[D]   [C]   [F]

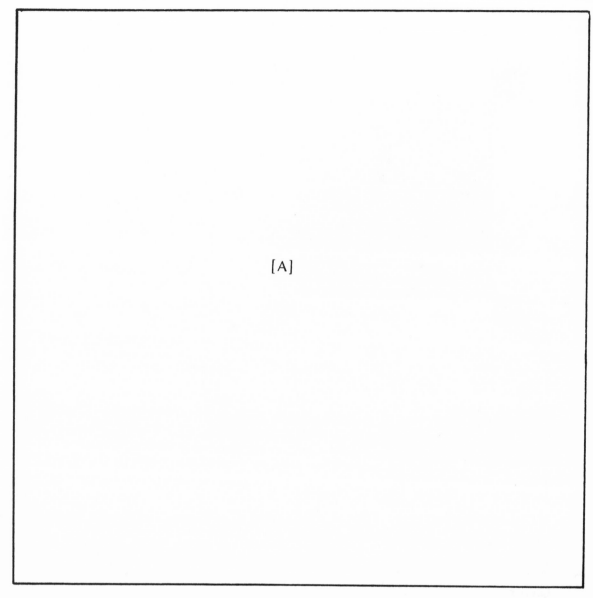

[A]

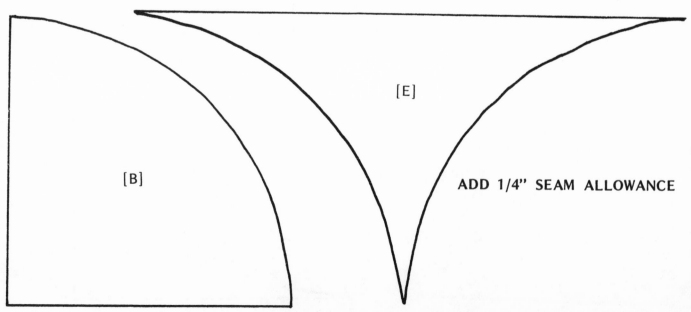

[B]

[E]

ADD 1/4" SEAM ALLOWANCE

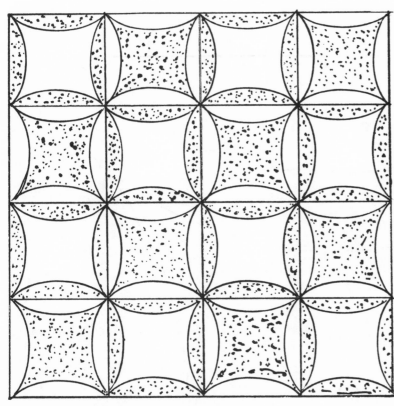

MODERATE

Quilt Size:	77" x 82-1/2"
Block Size:	5-1/2"
Blocks in Quilt:	210
	(14 across by 15 down)

Material:
4-1/2 yds. Light Color
4-1/2 yds. Dark Color

Pieces		per Block	per Quilt
A	1	Dark or Light	210
			(105 Dark)
			(105 Light)
B	4	Light or Dark	840
			(420 Dark)
			(420 Light)

in color p. 5

84. Robbing Peter to Pay Paul I

In this old favorite with quilters, any two harmonizing colors may be used. The pattern has also been called *Orange Peel* and *Dolly Madison's Workbox*.

   Sewing Instructions: Cut out pattern pieces, adding seam allowance. To set the quilt, follow the diagram, which shows sixteen blocks set together. Dark and light blocks are alternated.

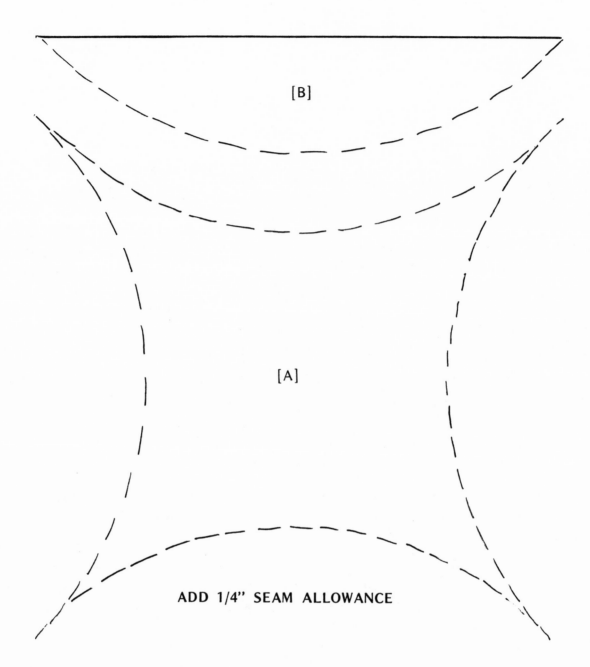

[B]

[A]

ADD 1/4" SEAM ALLOWANCE

[B]	[C]	[D]
[E]	[C]	[C]
[A]		

EASY

Quilt Size:	72" x 84"	
Block Size:	12"	
Blocks in Quilt:	42	
	(6 across by 7 down)	

Material:
   4 yds. Print
   4 yds. White

Pieces per Block			per Quilt
A	1	Print	42
B	4	White	168
C	12	White	504
	20	Print	840
D	4	White	168
E	4	White	168

in color p. 8

85. Robbing Peter to Pay Paul II

ADD 1/4" SEAM ALLOWANCE

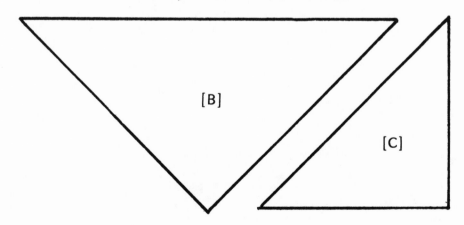
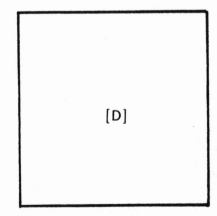

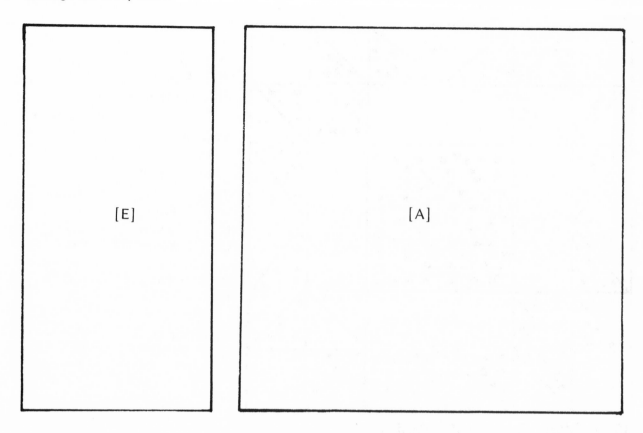

ADD 1/4" SEAM ALLOWANCE

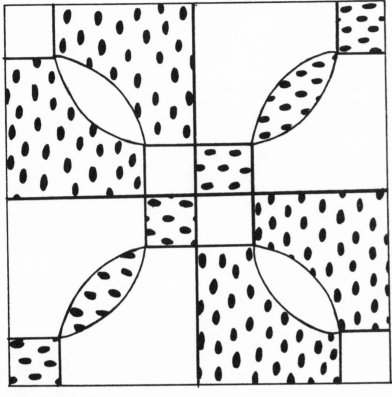

86. Rose Dream

MODERATE

Quilt Size:	85" x 102"
Block Size:	12"
Blocks in Quilt:	30
	(5 across by 6 down)

Material:
  5 yds. Pink
  5 yds. Pink Print

Pieces	**per Block**	**per Quilt**
A	2 Plain	60
	2 Print	60
B	4 Plain	120
	4 Print	120
C	4 Plain	120
	4 Print	120

Other Units:
18   Half Blocks
 4   Quarter Blocks

in color p. 5

Sewing Instructions: When completed the blocks are set diagonally. Begin at the left corner with a quarter block, and work across the top placing half blocks along the edges and a quarter block at each corner.

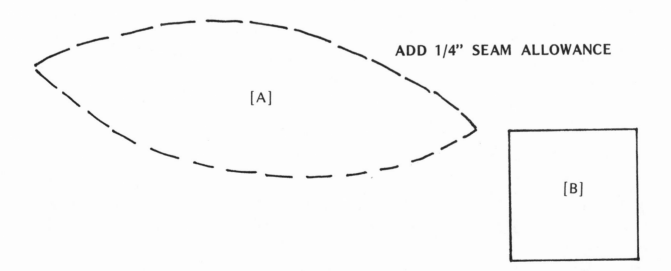

ADD 1/4" SEAM ALLOWANCE

[A]

[B]

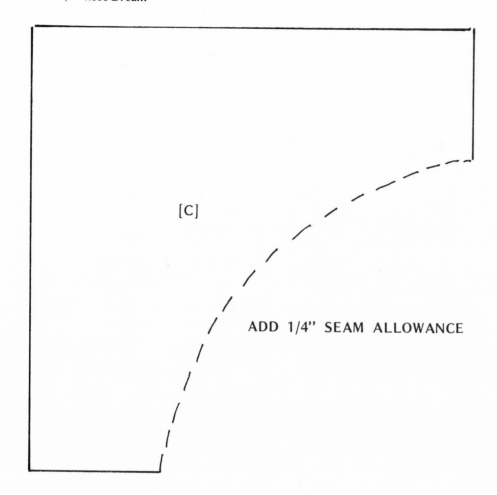

[C]

ADD 1/4" SEAM ALLOWANCE

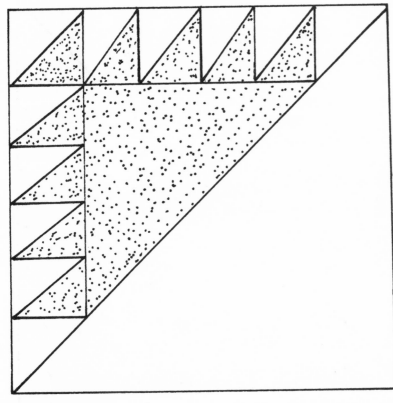

87. Sawtooth

EASY

Quilt Size:	90" x 105"
Block Size:	15"
Blocks in Quilt:	42
	(6 across by 7 down)

Material:
  8 yds. White
  6 yds. Print (scrap fabric)

Pieces per Block			per Quilt
A	11	White	462
	9	Print	378
B	1	Print	42
C	1	White	42

in color p. 10

The *Sawtooth* patterns date from at least the early 1800s, and there are many, many variations. *Kansas Troubles* is a variation of *Sawtooth.*

    Sewing Instructions: The pattern for Piece C is a 14-1/2" square, cut in half diagonally (pattern not shown). Be sure to add seam allowance when cutting. Space does not permit showing the entire pattern for Piece B. When drawing your pattern, merely extend the lines until they meet.

    This pattern makes up best if the same print is used for a diagonal row across the quilt. To piece it, join the outside triangles A into squares of print and plain; then join into strips. Stitch the strips to part B and then to part C to complete the block.

    Quilting: Quilt 1/8" from all seams. Extend the pieced lines into the plain side of the block and repeat the pattern. Fill in the center of the block with straight lines from the points of the small triangles.

ADD 1/4" SEAM ALLOWANCE

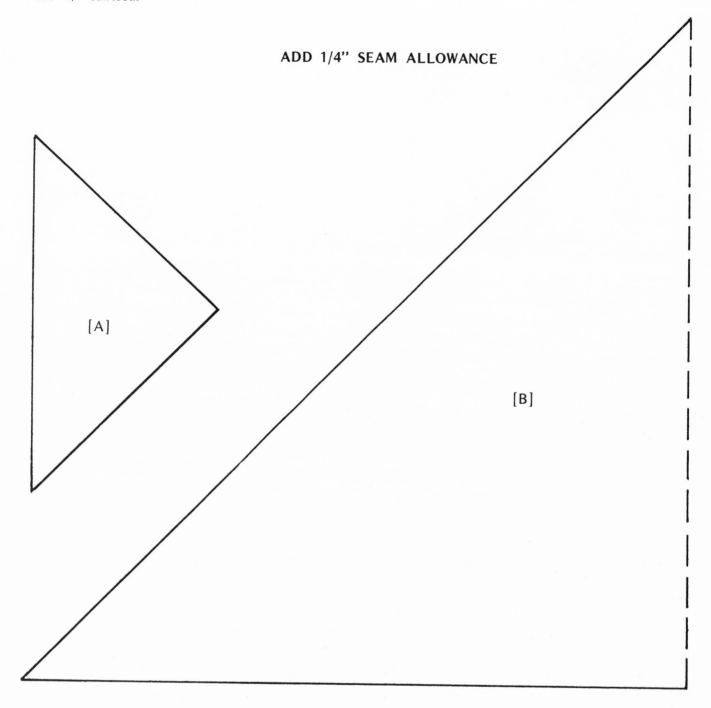

[A]

[B]

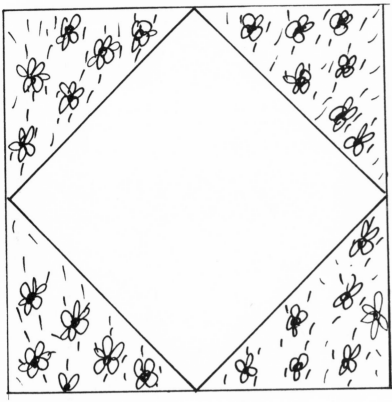

EASY

Quilt Size:		80" x 96"
Block Size:		8"
Blocks in Quilt:		120
		(10 across by 12 down)

Material:
   5 yds. Print
   5 yds. Plain

Pieces per Block		per Quilt
A	4 Print or Plain	480
		(240 Print)
		(240 Plain)
B	1 Plain or Print	120
		(60 Print)
		(60 Plain)

in color p. 10

88. Shoofly I

The distinctive characteristic of *Shoofly* patterns is the alternating of dark and light pieces from block to block. It has been popular throughout the years because of the changing optical illusion created in the finished top. *Ohio Star, Corn & Beans, Duck & Ducklings,* and *Churn Dash* have also been called *Shoofly*.

   Sewing Instructions: The first block begins with print Pieces A, the second block has plain Pieces A.

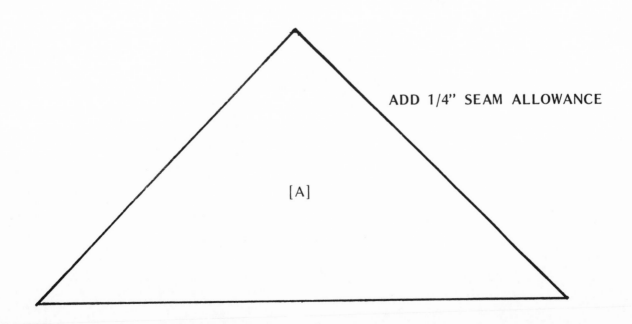

ADD 1/4" SEAM ALLOWANCE

[A]

[B]

ADD 1/4" SEAM ALLOWANCE

EASY

Quilt Size:	77" x 88"
Block Size:	11'
Blocks in Quilt:	56

(28 pieced, 28 plain; 7 across by 8 down)

Material: (36" fabric)
5-1/2 yds. White
3 yds. Color

Pieces per Block			per Quilt
A	4	White	112
	4	Color	112
B	4	White	112
	4	Color	112
C	4	Color	112

Other Units:
28   White Blocks, 11-1/2" square

in color p. 16

91. Spider Web

Sewing Instructions: Cut out pattern pieces, adding 1/4" seam allowance. Also cut out the 28 plain white blocks, 11" square, adding 1/4" seam allowance. Piece the block in the following manner:

Step 1

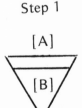

Piece 8 per block

Step 2

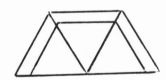

Sew units together

Step 3

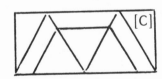

Add corner units

Setting the Quilt: Alternate the pieced blocks with plain white blocks.

Quilting: Quilt the pieced blocks with stitching 1/4" from all seams. To carry out the theme of the quilt, repeat the pieced pattern in the plain blocks.

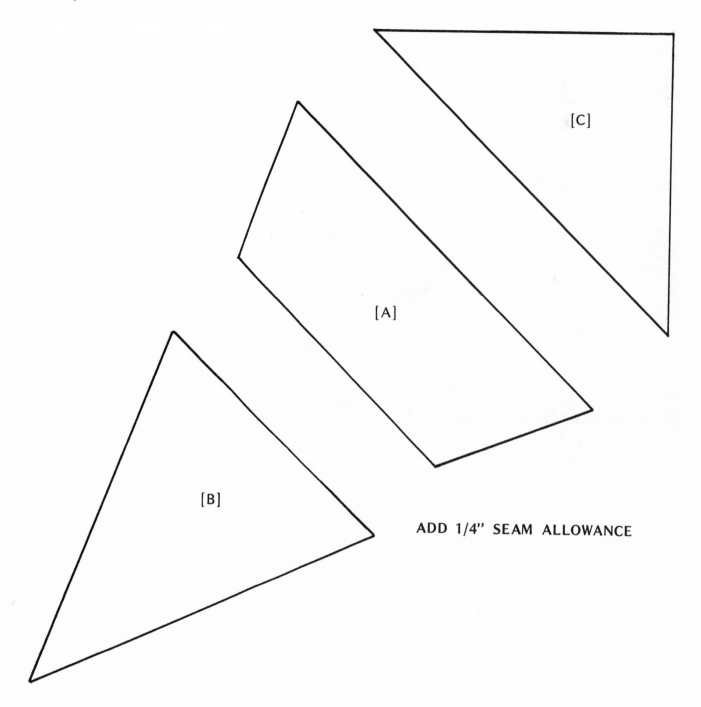

[C]

[A]

[B]

ADD 1/4" SEAM ALLOWANCE

92. Aunt Eliza's Star

EASY

Quilt Size:	75" x 90"	
Block Size:	15"	
Blocks in Quilt:	30	
	(5 across by 6 down)	

Material:
4-1/4 yds. White
1 yd. Red
1-1/4 yds. Blue

Pieces per Block			per Quilt
A	1	White	30
B	4	White	120
	4	Red	120
C	8	Blue	240
	4	White	120
D	4	White	120

in color p. 6

ADD 1/4" SEAM ALLOWANCE

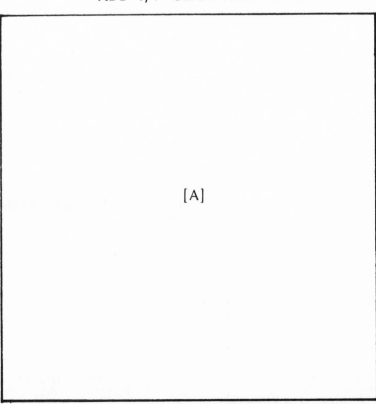

[A]

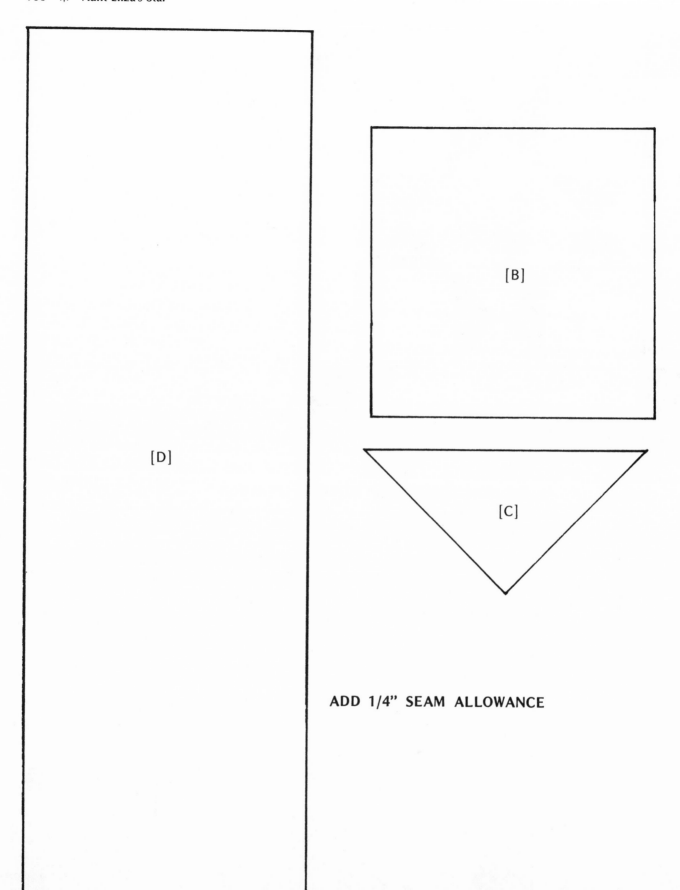

[D]

[B]

[C]

ADD 1/4" SEAM ALLOWANCE

93. Star of Bethlehem

DIFFICULT

Quilt Size: 76" x 90"
Block Size: 14"
Blocks in Quilt: 30
                (5 across by 6 down)

Material:
    4-2/3 yds. Green
    1-1/2 yds. Yellow
    2-1/2 yds. Pink
    1 yd. White
    3/4 yd. for border

Pieces		per Block	per Quilt
A	8	Pink	240
B	4	Yellow (inner star)	120
	4	Green (inner star)	120
	8	Green (outer edge)	240
			240
C	16	White	480
D	4	Green	120

Other Units:
    Border: 3" wide

in color p. 14

This color combination makes a lovely, soft quilt. There are several *Star of Bethlehem* patterns, but this is one of the favorites.

ADD 1/4" SEAM ALLOWANCE

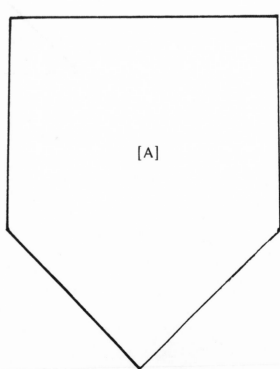

[A]

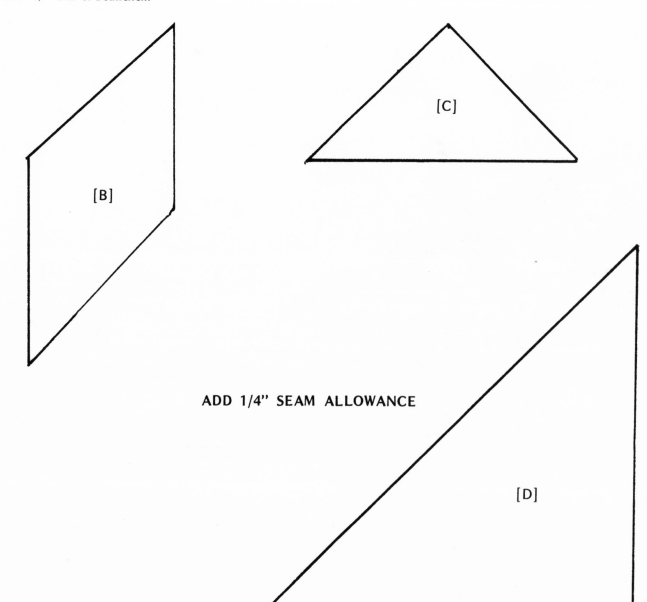

[B]

[C]

[D]

ADD 1/4" SEAM ALLOWANCE

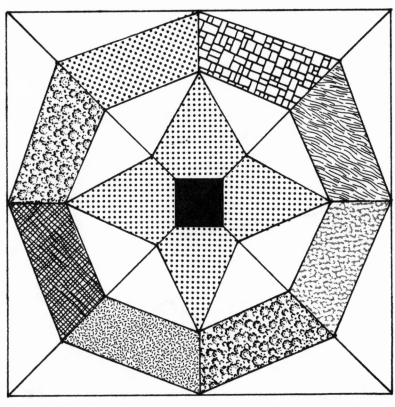

94. Star & Crown

MODERATE

Quilt Size:		80" x 90"
Block Size:		10"
Blocks in Quilt:		72
		(8 across by 9 down)

Material:
    8 yds. White
    1/4 yd. Orange
    Assorted Scraps of print and plain
    2-1/4 Light Print

Pieces per Block			per Quilt
A	8	White	576
B	8	Assorted	576
C	8	White	576
D	4	Light Print	288
E	1	Orange	72

in color p. 16

Sewing Instructions: Cut out pattern pieces, adding 1/4" seam allowance. To assemble the block, follow the diagram, and join as follows: A to B to C. You will need eight such units. Join two of these assembled units to each side of part D. Join these assembled units to Piece E.

Border: No border is necessary; just bind off with 1/2" binding around the edges.

Quilting: Quilt 1/8" from all seams.

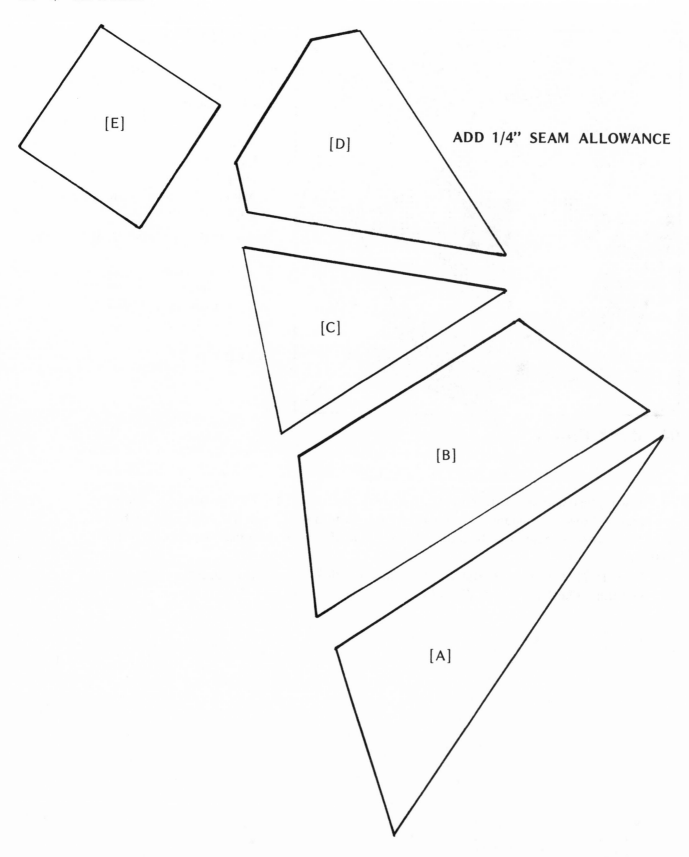

ADD 1/4" SEAM ALLOWANCE

[E]

[D]

[C]

[B]

[A]

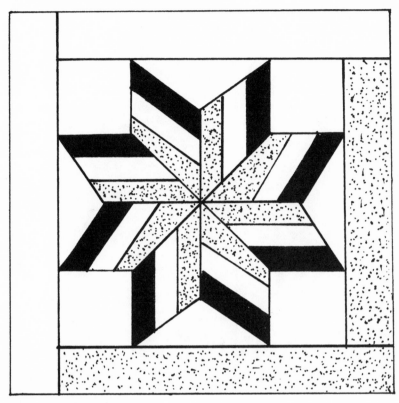

95. Liberty Star

DIFFICULT

Quilt Size: 86" x 103"
Block Size: 15"
Blocks in Quilt: 20
(4 across by 5 down)

Material:
8 yds. White
2 yds. Red
2 yds. Blue

Pieces per Block			per Quilt
A	8	Red	160
	8	White	160
	8	Blue	160
B	4	White	80
C	4	White	80
2		Red Strips, 1-1/2" wide	40
2		Blue Strips, 1-1/2" wide	40

Other Units:
Border: 2 Red Strips, 3" wide;
2 White Strips, 3" wide;
2 Blue Strips, 3" wide

in color p. 1

This pattern was drafted from a quilt made in 1855.

Sewing Instructions: Piece the eight points of the star using red, white, and blue Pieces A, with the colors placed as shown in the drawing. When each point has been sewn, assemble them into the star. Add parts Pieces B and C to complete the block. A 2" border is sewn around each block as shown.

You can also piece the star and then applique it to a 15-1/2" block.

Border: The border consists of three strips, one red, one white, and one blue, each 3" wide. Place the white strip first, then the red, then the blue.

Quilting: The quilting is simple outline quilting, 1/8" from each seam.

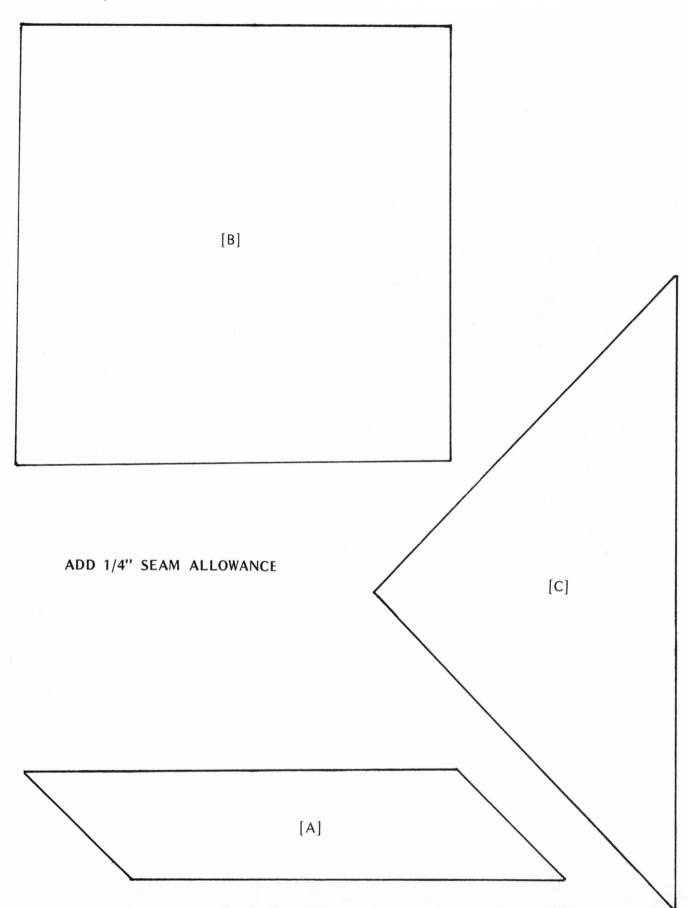

[B]

ADD 1/4" SEAM ALLOWANCE

[C]

[A]

EASY

Quilt Size:	84" x 96"	
Block Size:	12"	
Blocks in Quilt:	56	
	(7 across by 8 down)	

Material:
   5-3/4 yds. Blue
   5-3/4 yds. White

Pieces per Block			per Quilt
A	2	Blue	112
	2	White	112
B	4	Blue	224
	4	White	224

in color p. 8

96. Northern Star

This pattern can be made up in any two colors, but blue and white are most appropriate to the name. You can use either a plain or a print fabric.

   Sewing Instructions: Cut out pattern units, adding 1/4" seam allowance. This is a simple block to assemble: two pieces of light and dark A and two pieces of light and dark B as shown in the illustration. To set the blocks together, follow the diagram.
   Border: No border is required; just bind off edges.
   Quilting: Quilt 1/8" from all seams.

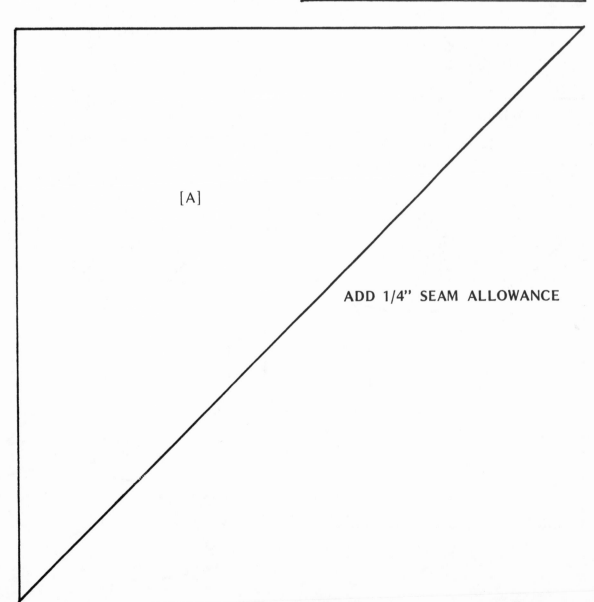

[B]

[A]

ADD 1/4" SEAM ALLOWANCE

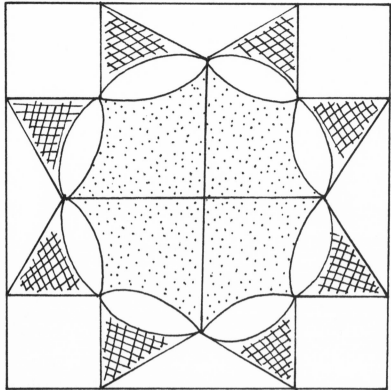

97. French Star

Sewing Instructions: Top is set with blocks on the diagonal alternating with plain blocks.

DIFFICULT

Quilt Size: 78" x 78"
Block Size: 11"
Blocks in Quilt: 41
    (25 pieced, 16 plain; 5 across by 5 down)

Material:
    6-1/2 yds. White
    2 yds. Yellow
    1-1/2 yds. Orange

Pieces per Block			per Quilt
A	8	White	200
B	4	Orange	100
C	4	White	100
D	8	Yellow	200
E	4	White	100

Other Units:
16   Blocks, 13" square
16   Half Blocks
 4   Quarter Blocks

in color p. 4

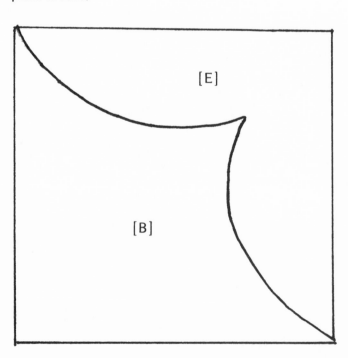

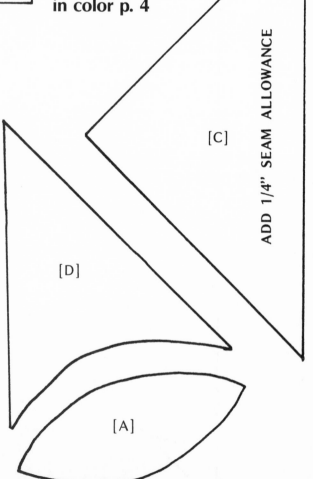

ADD 1/4" SEAM ALLOWANCE

ADD 1/4" SEAM ALLOWANCE

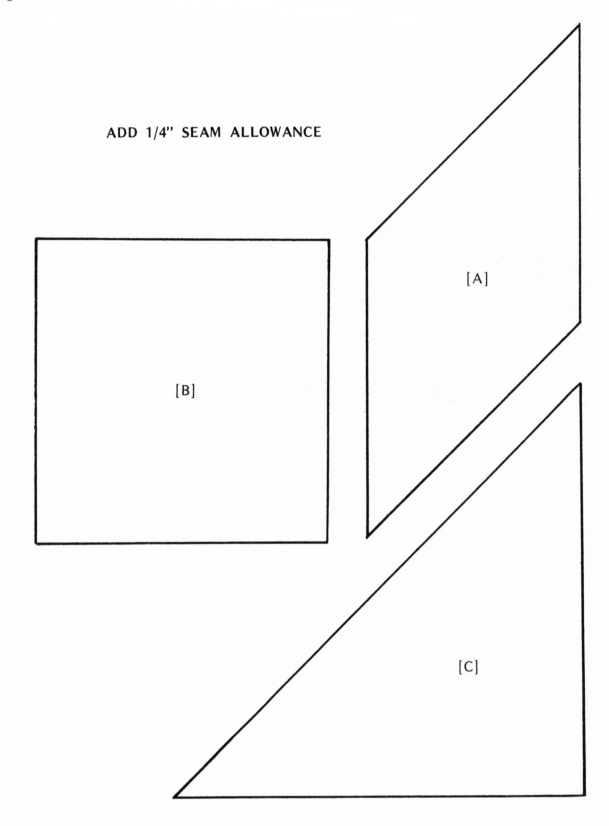

EASY

Quilt Size:	72" x 84"
Block Size:	12"
Blocks in Quilt:	42
	(6 across by 7 down)

Material:
   5-1/2 yds. Light Color
   3 yds. Dark Color

Pieces per Block			per Quilt
A	4	Light	82
		or Dark	82
	1	Dark	21
		or Light	21
B	8	Dark	168
		or Light	168
	8	Light	168
		or Dark	168

in color p. 9

99. Ohio Star

This pattern dates from the early 1800s and is also known as *Variable Star* or *Shoofly*.

    Sewing Instructions: Cut out pattern pieces, adding seam allowance. Light blocks are alternated with dark in setting the quilt, as in other *Shoofly* patterns.

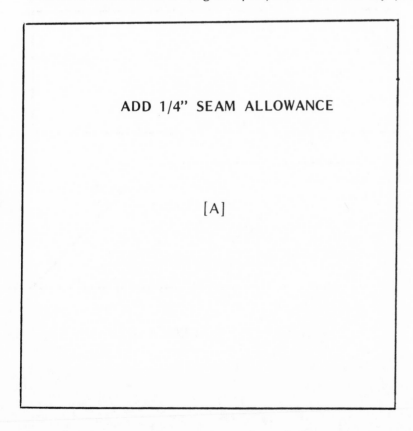

ADD 1/4" SEAM ALLOWANCE

[A]

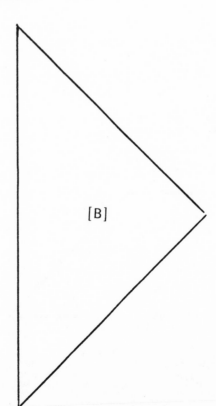

[B]

EASY

Quilt Size:	81" x 99"	
Block Size:	9"	
Blocks in Quilt:	99	
	(9 across by 11 down)	

Material:
  6-3/4 yds. White
  6-1/4 yds. Color

Pieces per Block			per Quilt
A	1	White	99
	4	Color	396
B	4	White	396
C	8	White	792
D	8	Color	792

in color p. 11

100. Stonemason's Puzzle

   Sewing Instructions: Cut out pattern pieces and follow diagram. Blocks are set side by side, with no strips or plain blocks, for an allover pattern.

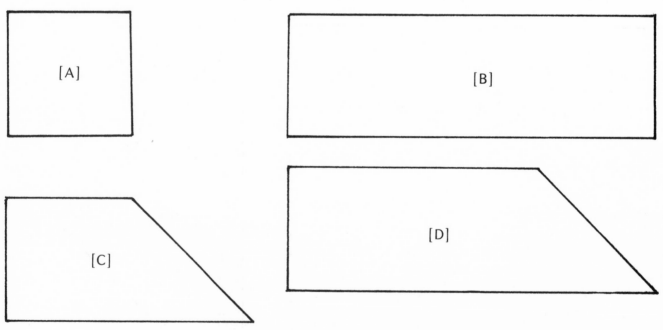

ADD 1/4" SEAM ALLOWANCE

EASY

Quilt Size:	80" x 100"

This pattern is pieced in rows rather than blocks. There are 32 rows across and 40 rows down.

Material:
6 yds. Dark (Black)
6 yds. Light (Red)

Pieces Required:
A   640 Light
       640 Dark
B   32 Light
        32 Dark

in color p. 14

101. Streak of Lightning

This pattern is an adaptation of the old *Streak O'Lightnin'* pattern. In the hands of the Pennsylvania Dutch women during the 1800s, this pattern made a strong graphic statement. Using black and red or red and blue, the finished quilts look as modern as any made today.

    Sewing Instructions: Starting with Piece B, add alternate color Piece A, then continue alternating dark and light Piece A in a strip forty pieces long. Add a part B to finish the strip. As a row is completed, add it to the previous row.

    Border: A plain strip border is all that is necessary.

    Quilting: Quilt 1/8" from all seams.

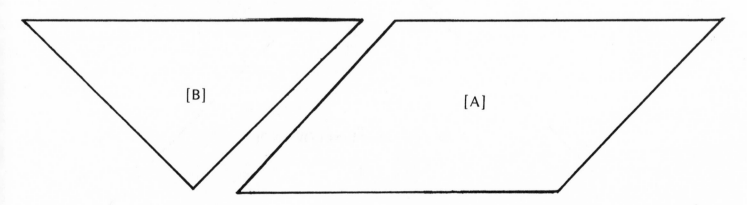

[B]   [A]

ADD 1/4" SEAM ALLOWANCE

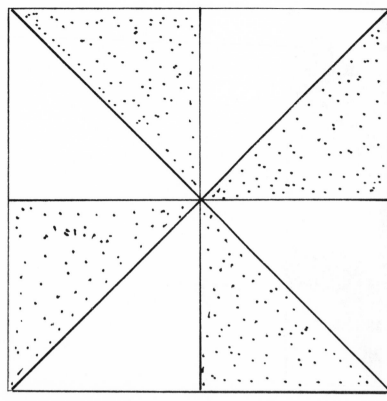

EASY

Quilt Size:	80" x 90"
Block Size:	10"
Blocks in Quilt:	72
	(8 across by 9 down)

Material:
  5-1/2 yds. White
  5-1/2 yds. Print

Pieces per Block		per Quilt
A	4 White	288
	4 Print	288

in color p. 8

102. Sugar Bowl

This is a very simple pattern to piece. As evidence of its popularity, it has many names. Known as the *Fly* in Ohio, *Kathy's Ramble* in New York, *Crow's Foot* in Maryland and *Fan Mill* in Pennsylvania, the most obvious name is *Pinwheel.*

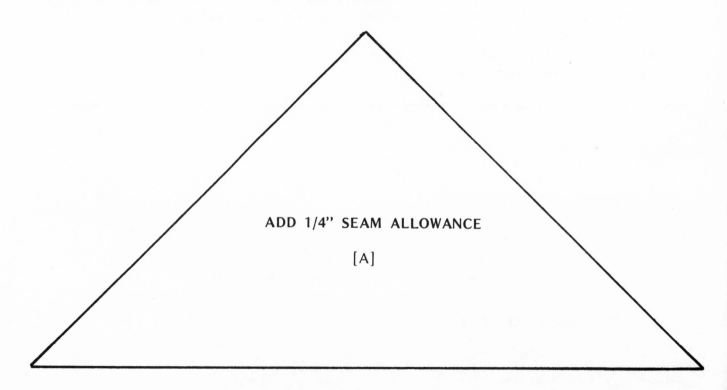

ADD 1/4" SEAM ALLOWANCE

[A]

MODERATE

Quilt Size:	85" x 85"	
Block Size:	15-1/2" x 12-1/2"	
Blocks in Quilt:	30	
	(5 across by 6 down)	

Material:
2-1/2 yds. Blue
5-1/2 yds. White

Pieces per Block			per Quilt
A	6	Blue	180
	4	White	120
B	2	White	60
C	5	White	150

Other Units:
Border: 5" wide

in color p. 6

103. Sugar Loaf

This pattern derives from the days when sugar came in loaves wrapped in blue paper.

Sewing Instructions: Cut out pattern pieces, adding seam allowance. To assemble, break block into three units.

This quilt also makes quite a pretty statement if dark blue and light blue fabrics are used.

Border: Add a 5" border around the quilt.

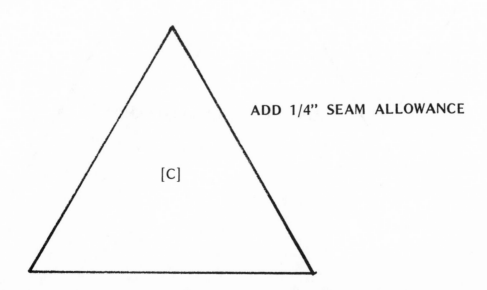

ADD 1/4" SEAM ALLOWANCE

[C]

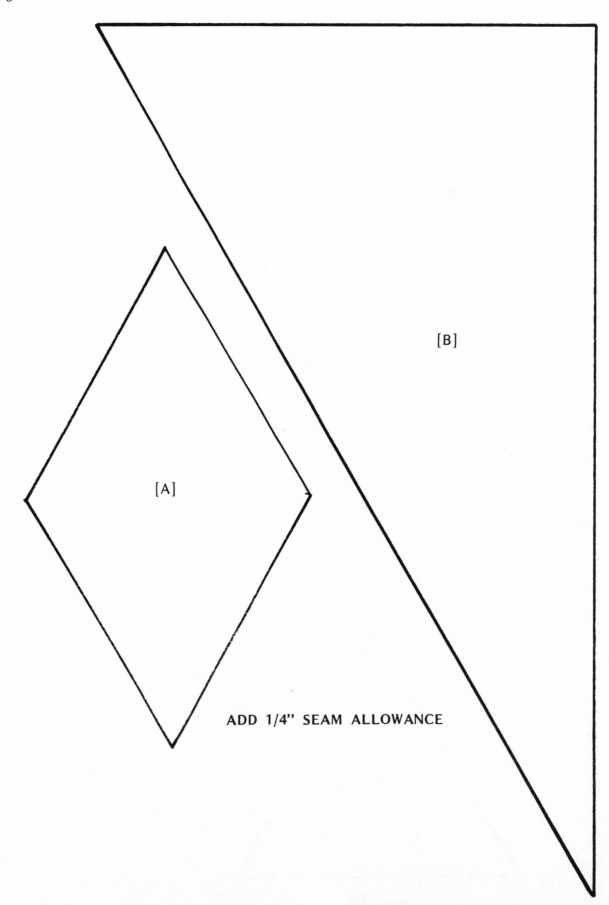

[B]

[A]

ADD 1/4" SEAM ALLOWANCE

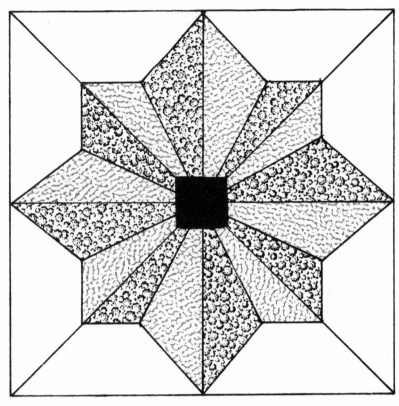

104. Sunbeam

MODERATE

Quilt Size:	85" square
Block Size:	12"
Blocks in Quilt:	41

(25 pieced, 16 plain; 5 across by 5 down)

Material:
1-1/2 yds. Orange
1 yd. Red
1 yd. Yellow
5-2/3 yds. White

Pieces	per Block		per Quilt
A	1	Orange	25
B	4	Red	100
	4	Yellow	
		(reversed)	100
C	8	White	200
D	4	Yellow	
		(reversed)	100
	4	Red	100

Other Units:
16 Plain Blocks, 12-1/2" square
16 Half Blocks
 4 Quarter Blocks

in color p. 4

ADD 1/4" SEAM ALLOWANCE

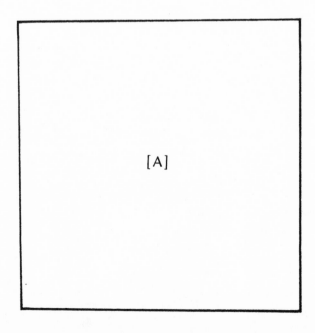

[A]

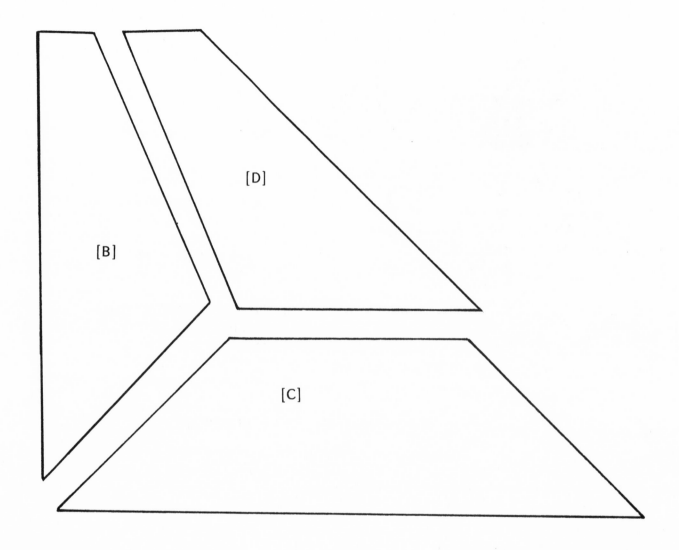

[D]

[B]

[C]

ADD 1/4" SEAM ALLOWANCE

105. Sunflower

MODERATE

Quilt Size:	91" x 109"
Block Size:	17"
Blocks in Quilt:	30
	(5 across by 6 down)

Material:
8 yds. White
1-1/2 yds. Color (dividing strips)
Assorted Prints (flower petals)
1/4 yd. Yellow or Brown (center)

Pieces per Block			per Quilt
A	1	Brown	
		or Yellow	30
B	20	Assorted	600
Background Block,			
	18" square		30

Other Units:
24 Lattice Strips, 1-1/2" x 18"
5 Lattice Strips, 1-1/2" x 91-1/2"

in color p. 16

Sewing Instructions: Cut out background block 18" square. (This allows for a 1/2" seam.) Cut out design pieces, adding 1/4" seam allowance. Seam the B pieces together, then applique them to the background block. Applique the center in place.

Setting the Quilt: Cut 1-1/2" x 18" strips. Sew the strips to the side of your first block; then stitch to second block. Continue across for five blocks. A single strip, 1" wide by the width of the finished strip, can then be cut and stitched to the bottom of the blocks. Continue in this manner until quilt is finished. Add a 1" strip to outer edges.

Quilting: Quilt 1/8" from all seams. For the background, fill in with a circular pattern approximately 1/2" apart.

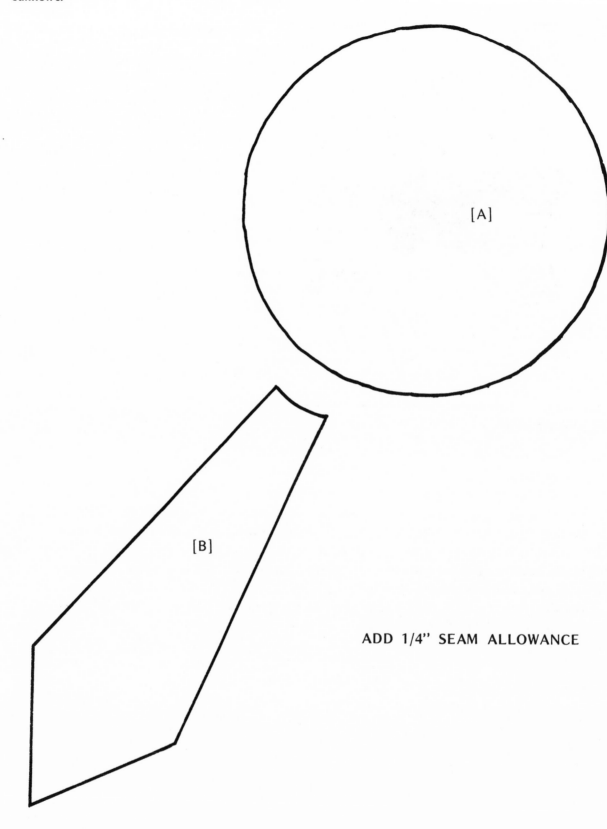

[A]

[B]

ADD 1/4" SEAM ALLOWANCE

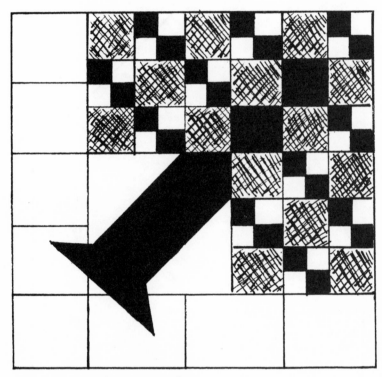

106. Tree of Temptation

EASY

Quilt Size:	92" x 92"
Block Size:	15"
Blocks in Quilt:	25
	(4 across by 4 down)

Material:
  1 yd. Brown
  2-1/2 yds. Red
  1-3/4 yds. Green Print
  5 yds. White

Pieces per Block			per Quilt
A	1	Brown	25
B	14	Green	350
	2	Brown	50
C	22	White	550
	22	Red	550
D	1	White	25
E	9	White	225

Other Units:
12   Half Blocks
 4   Quarter Blocks
     Border: 4" wide Strips

in color p. 14

Sewing Instructions: This is a simple pattern to put together. First assemble the small red and white blocks to form squares as shown. Then sew these to the green print squares. Add the large square to the corner, and then the outside squares to finish the block. When this has been completed, applique Piece A to the finished block.

Setting the Quilt: Make a pattern 14" square, and cut it in half diagonally. Adding seam allowance, cut out 12 half squares. Cut the pattern in half again, and cut out 4 quarter squares. Starting with a quarter block, set the blocks together diagonally.

Border: Use a strip of white, 4" wide and long enough to go around the quilt top.

Quilting: Quilt 1/8" from each seam. Fill in the white strips with diagonal lines or diamonds.

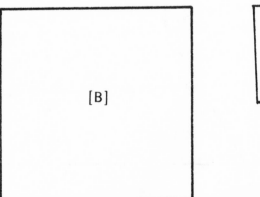

[B]

[C]

ADD 1/4" SEAM ALLOWANCE

ADD 1/4" SEAM ALLOWANCE

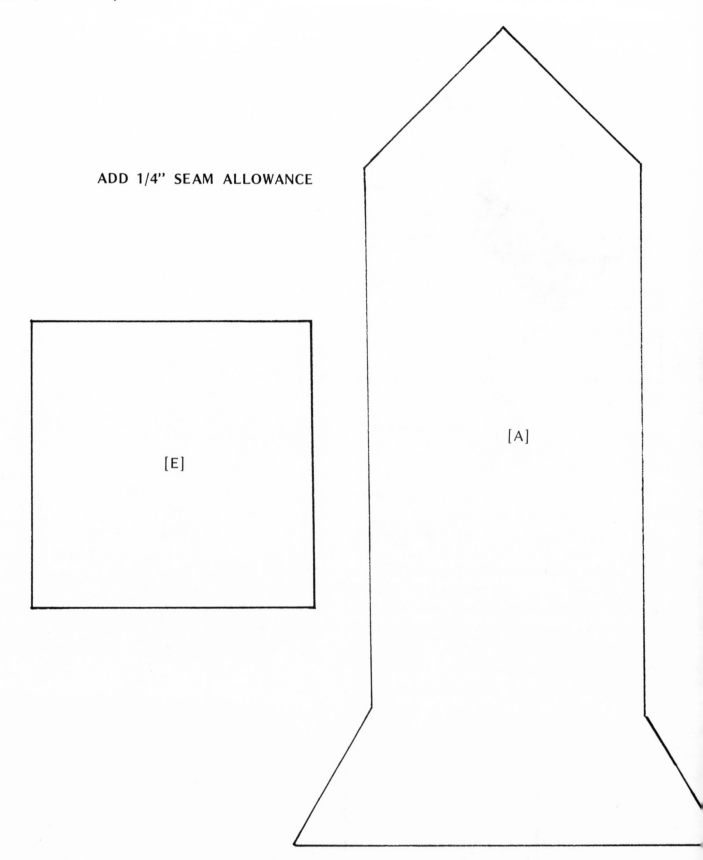

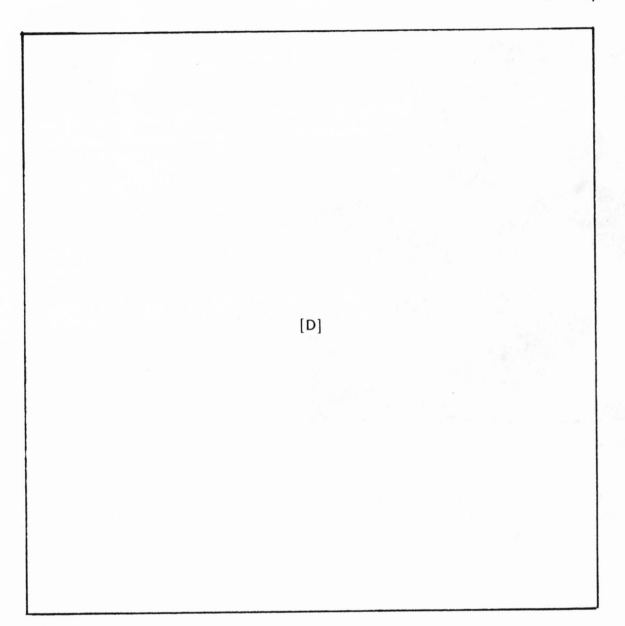

[D]

ADD 1/4" SEAM ALLOWANCE

EASY

Quilt Size:	76-1/2" x 93-1/2"
Block Size:	8-1/2"
Blocks in Quilt:	99

(45 pieced, 44 plain; 9 across by 11 down)

Material:
5-1/2 yds. White
3-1/2 yds. Color (Red)

Pieces per Block			per Quilt
A	4	White	180
	4	Red	180
B	8	White	360
	8	Red	360

in color p. 4

107. Swastika

The *Swastika* pattern has long been a favorite with quilters.

It is known as *Fly Foot* in Ohio, and *Catch Me if You Can, Battle Ax of Thor, Chinese 10,000 Perfections, Heart's Seal, Favorite of the Peruvians, Mound Builders, Wind Power of the Osages,* and *Pure Symbol of Right Doctrine.*

ADD 1/4" SEAM ALLOWANCE

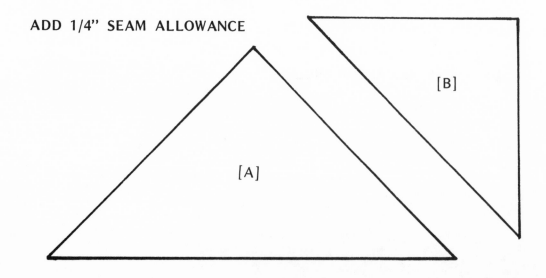

108. Triple Sunflower

The *Triple Sunflower* is well known to all quilt lovers. It is strongly associated with the State of Kansas.

MODERATE

Quilt Size:	93" x 108"
Block Size:	12"
Blocks in Quilt:	42
	(6 across by 7 down)

Material:
  2-1/2 yds. Yellow Print
  3 yds. Green
  6 yds. White
  2-1/2 yds. Orange or Yellow, Plain
  1 yd. Brown
  3 yds. for Lattice Strips and Border

Pieces per Block			per Quilt
A	1	Brown	42
B	4	Print	168
	4	Plain	168
C	4	White	168
D	4	White	168
E	2	Green	84
F	1	Green	42
G	2	Green	84
H	1	White	42

Other Units:
72 Lattice Strips, 3" wide
     Border: 3" wide

in color p. 3

Sewing Instructions: Piece the flower squares, and then join four blocks as shown to form the whole block. Applique the leaves and stems in place. The quilt is set with 3" lattice strips between each block and with a 3" border.

ADD 1/4" SEAM ALLOWANCE

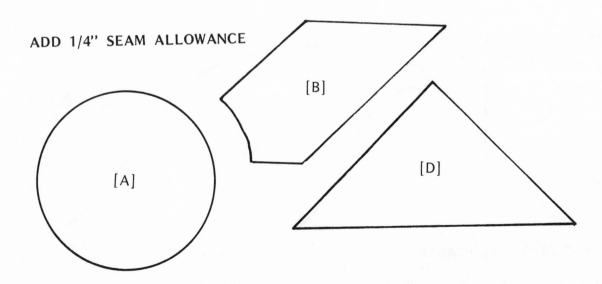

[H]

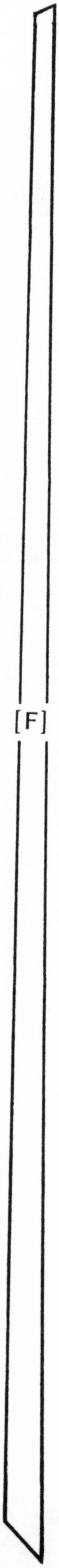

[F]

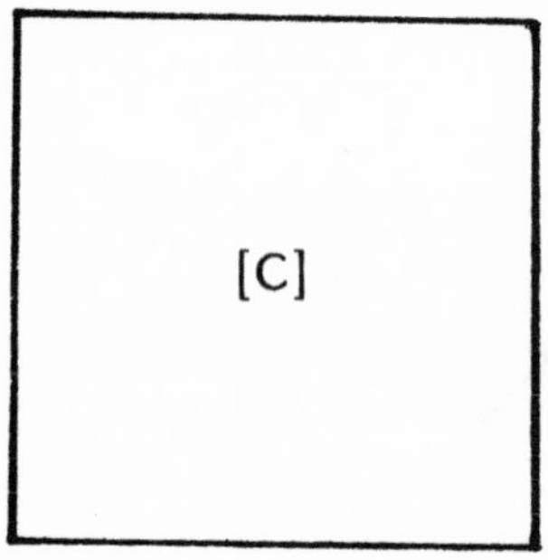

[C]

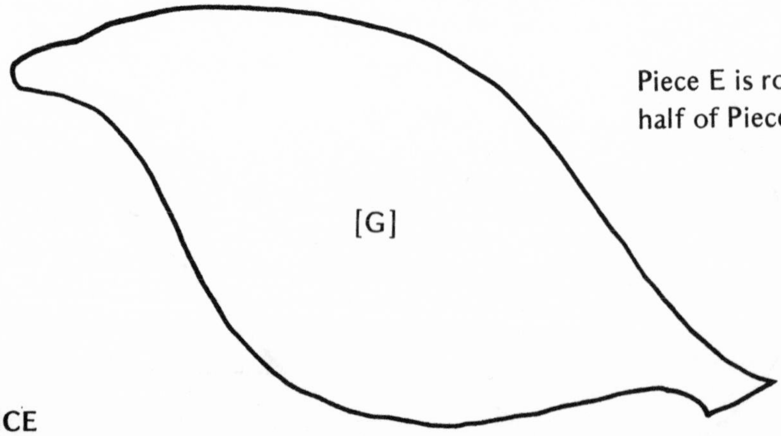

[G]

Piece E is roughly
half of Piece F

ADD 1/4" SEAM ALLOWANCE

109. Tumbler

EASY

This pattern really needs no instructions. It is a scrap pattern worked across in rows. Just continue adding units until the quilt is the size you want it to be.

You can ignore the individual units, and do an overall quilting design on the top.

in color p. 13

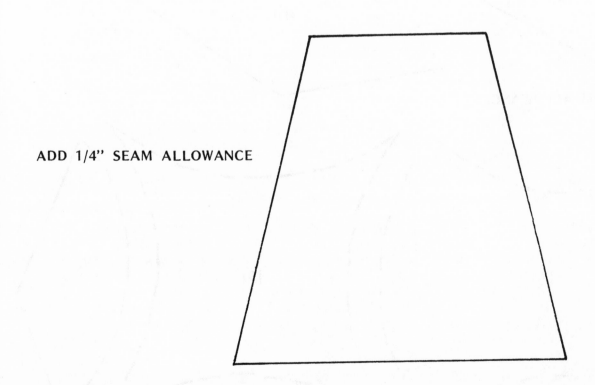

ADD 1/4" SEAM ALLOWANCE

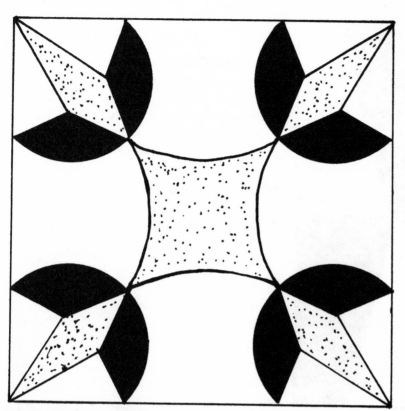

110. Turkey Tracks

MODERATE

Quilt Size:	63" x 81"
Block Size:	9"
Blocks in Quilt:	63

(32 pieced, 31 plain; 7 across by 9 down)

Material:
1-1/4 yds. Yellow Print
1 yd. Red
6-1/2 yds. White

Pieces per Block			per Quilt
A	4	White	128
B	1	Yellow Print	32
C	8	Red	256
D	4	Yellow Print	128
E	8	White	256

in color p. 4

Sewing Instructions: Blocks are set in rows, alternating with plain white, 7 across and 9 down. To make a bigger quilt, simply add rows.

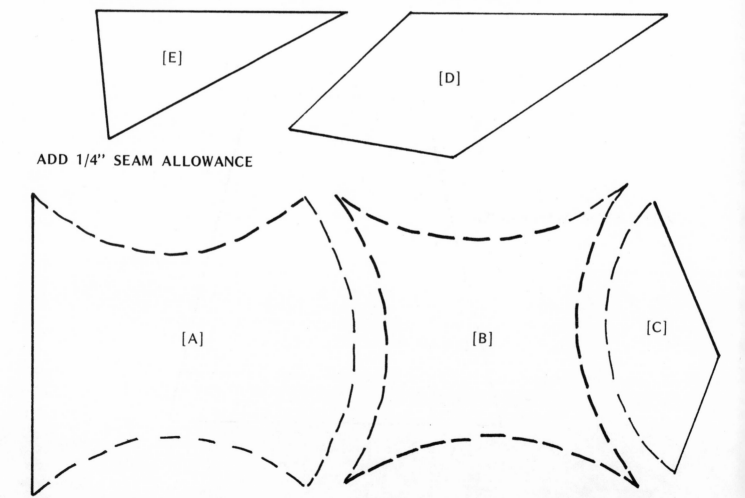

ADD 1/4" SEAM ALLOWANCE

[E]

[D]

[A]

[B]

[C]

MODERATE

Quilt Size:	93" x 93"	
Block Size:	12"	
Blocks in Quilt:	36	
	(6 across by 6 down)	

Material:
   6 yds. White
   5-1/2 yds. Assorted Prints and Solids

Pieces per Block			per Quilt
A	1	White	36
B	24	White	864
C	12	Solid	432
	4	White	144
D	4	Print	144

Other Units:
   Lattice Strips, 3" x 12"
   Border: 3" wide

in color p. 10

111. Wild Goose Chase I

This pattern dates back to at least 1847. At that time it was called *Geese in Flight*.

ADD 1/4" SEAM ALLOWANCE

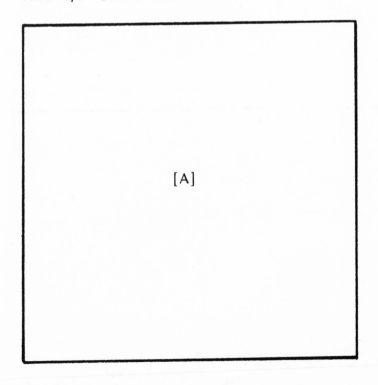

[A]

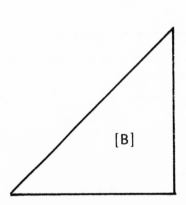

[B]

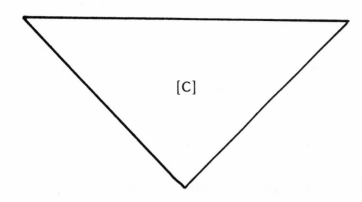

[C]

ADD 1/4" SEAM ALLOWANCE

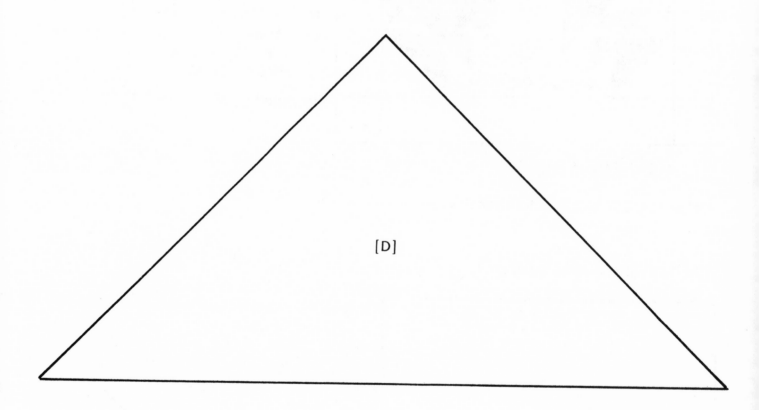

[D]

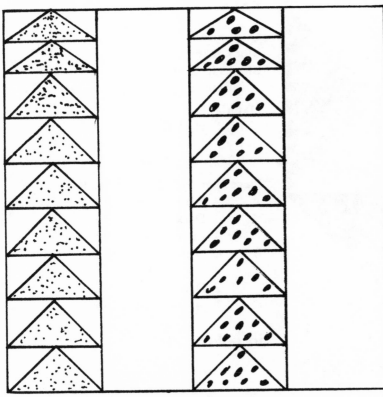

EASY

Quilt Size: 70" x 85"

Material:
   3-3/8 yds. White
   2-3/8 yds. Dark
   3/8 yd. each Seven Different Prints

Pattern Units:
A   28 Each Print
      7 White Strips, 6-1/2" x 85"
      6 Dark Strips, 5" x 85"

in color p. 11

112. Wild Goose Chase II

The quilt from which this pattern was taken was made in 1815. The pattern is very well known, but the method used for making this quilt is a little different than usual. Variations date back to at least 1785.

    Sewing Instructions: Cut out the strips as listed above. Cut out the 28 A pieces from each fabric. (Seam allowances have already been made.) Place the triangles on the white strip, overlapping each triangle slightly. Stitch in place. After the strips are completed, sew them to the dark strips, alternating applique, dark, applique, until the quilt is complete.

    Border: A simple binding is used to finish the edges of the quilt.

    Quilting: Quilt around each triangle. The long strips offer a good surface for the use of a rope pattern or simple diagonal squares.

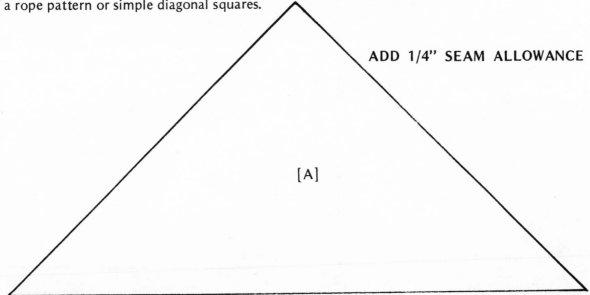

ADD 1/4" SEAM ALLOWANCE

[A]

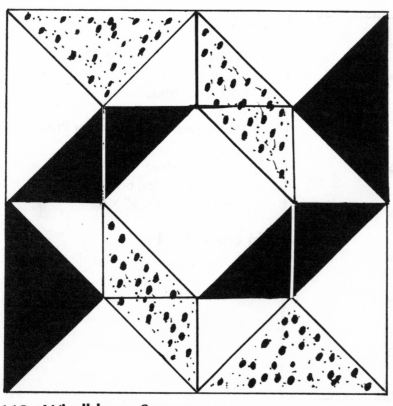

in color p. 10

EASY

Quilt Size:	72" x 81"
Block Size:	9"
Blocks in Quilt:	72

    (36 pieced, 36 plain; 8 across by 9 down)

Material:
1 yd. Dark Color
1 yd. Light Color
5-1/2 yds. White

Pieces	per Block		per Quilt
A	4	White	144
	4	Dark	144
	4	Light	144
B	4	White	144
	2	Light	72
	2	Dark	72
C	1	White	36

113. Windblown Square

This is also known as *Balkan Puzzle*.

ADD 1/4" SEAM ALLOWANCE

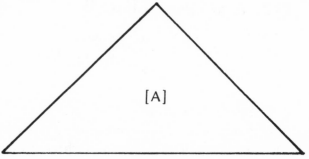

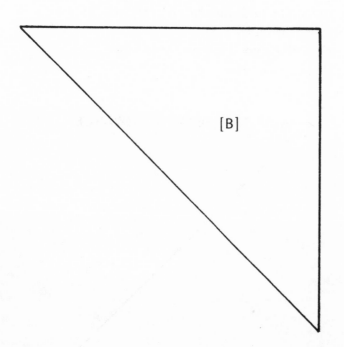

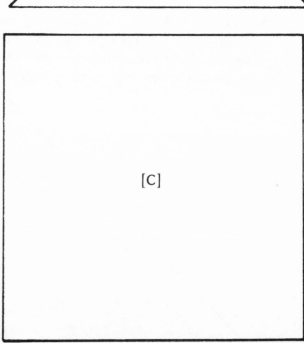

[A]

[B]

[C]

MODERATE

Quilt Size:	92" x 110"
Block Size:	18"
Blocks in Quilt:	20
	(4 across by 5 down)

Material:
   3 yds. Yellow
   3 yds. Green Print
   2-3/4 yds. Red Print
   3-1/2 yds. Color (border)

Pieces per Block			per Quilt
A	4	Yellow	80
B	16	Green Print	320
	16	Red Print	320
C	12	Yellow	240
	4	Green Print	80

Other Units:
   Border: 10" wide

in color p. 13

114. Wood Lily

This pattern was first published in the *Kansas City Star* in 1936. Their suggested color scheme is shown here. Feel free to change the colors to suit yourself.

   Sewing Instructions: Cut out pattern units, adding 1/4" seam allowance. By following the diagram, you should have no trouble in piecing the blocks.

   Border: Cut a border 10" wide to go around the quilt.

   Quilting: Quilt 1/8" from all seams. The border area gives lots of room for an elaborate quilting design. You might try a scalloped feather design with straight lines 1/2" apart running down to the feather edge.

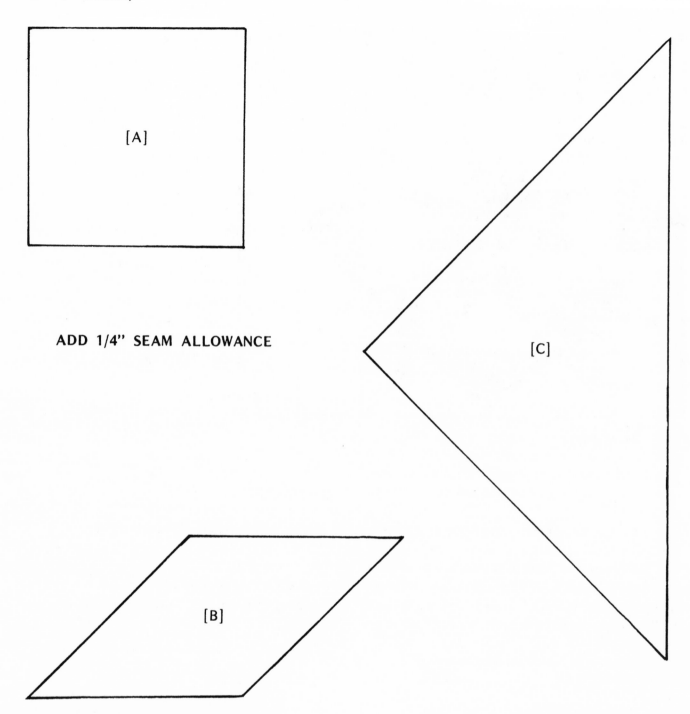

ADD 1/4" SEAM ALLOWANCE

[A]

[B]

[C]

MODERATE

Quilt Size:	84" x 96"	
Block Size:	12"	
Blocks in Quilt:	56	
	(7 across by 8 down)	

Material:
  7 yds. Dark Color
  7 yds. Light Color

Pieces per Block			per Quilt
A	8	Light	448
	8	Dark	448
B	8	Light	448
	8	Dark	448
C	2	Light	112
	2	Dark	112

in color p. 8

115. World Without End

This pattern, dating from the early 1800s, is also known as *Golden Wedding Ring*. It may be made up in white and one color or in two harmonizing colors. The choices are unlimited. Each block contains four smaller blocks set together. The lines are all straight but appear to be curved when the pattern is completed.

Sewing Instructions: Cut out pattern units, adding 1/4" seam allowance. Following the diagram for color, stitch Piece B to Piece C. Add Piece A, and continue around until the smaller block is finished. Piece four such blocks, alternating colors, and stitch together to complete a 12" block. When all blocks are completed, set them together 7 blocks across and 8 blocks down.

Border: No border is necessary; just bind off the edges.

Quilting: Quilt 1/8" on each side of all seams. No more elaborate design is necessary.

ADD 1/4" SEAM ALLOWANCE

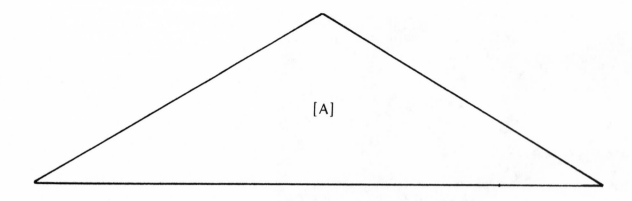

ADD 1/4" SEAM ALLOWANCE

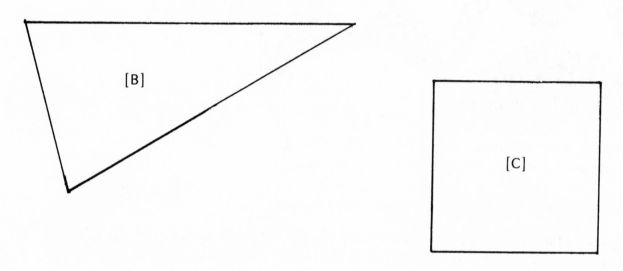

METRIC EQUIVALENCY CHART

MM—MILLIMETRES   CM—CENTIMETRES

INCHES TO MILLIMETRES AND CENTIMETRES

INCHES	MM	CM	INCHES	CM	INCHES	CM
⅛	3	0.3	9	22.9	30	76.2
¼	6	0.6	10	25.4	31	78.7
⅜	10	1.0	11	27.9	32	81.3
½	13	1.3	12	30.5	33	83.8
⅝	16	1.6	13	33.0	34	86.4
¾	19	1.9	14	35.6	35	88.9
⅞	22	2.2	15	38.1	36	91.4
1	25	2.5	16	40.6	37	94.0
1¼	32	3.2	17	43.2	38	96.5
1½	38	3.8	18	45.7	39	99.1
1¾	44	4.4	19	48.3	40	101.6
2	51	5.1	20	50.8	41	104.1
2½	64	6.4	21	53.3	42	106.7
3	76	7.6	22	55.9	43	109.2
3½	89	8.9	23	58.4	44	111.8
4	102	10.2	24	61.0	45	114.3
4½	114	11.4	25	63.5	46	116.8
5	127	12.7	26	66.0	47	119.4
6	152	15.2	27	68.6	48	121.9
7	178	17.8	28	71.1	49	124.5
8	203	20.3	29	73.7	50	127.0

YARDS TO METRES

YARDS	METRES	YARDS	METRES	YARDS	METRES	YARDS	METRES	YARDS	METRES
⅛	0.11	2⅛	1.94	4⅛	3.77	6⅛	5.60	8⅛	7.43
¼	0.23	2¼	2.06	4¼	3.89	6¼	5.72	8¼	7.54
⅜	0.34	2⅜	2.17	4⅜	4.00	6⅜	5.83	8⅜	7.66
½	0.46	2½	2.29	4½	4.11	6½	5.94	8½	7.77
⅝	0.57	2⅝	2.40	4⅝	4.23	6⅝	6.06	8⅝	7.89
¾	0.69	2¾	2.51	4¾	4.34	6¾	6.17	8¾	8.00
⅞	0.80	2⅞	2.63	4⅞	4.46	6⅞	6.29	8⅞	8.12
1	0.91	3	2.74	5	4.57	7	6.40	9	8.23
1⅛	1.03	3⅛	2.86	5⅛	4.69	7⅛	6.52	9⅛	8.34
1¼	1.14	3¼	2.97	5¼	4.80	7¼	6.63	9¼	8.46
1⅜	1.26	3⅜	3.09	5⅜	4.91	7⅜	6.74	9⅜	8.57
1½	1.37	3½	3.20	5½	5.03	7½	6.86	9½	8.69
1⅝	1.49	3⅝	3.31	5⅝	5.14	7⅝	6.97	9⅝	8.80
1¾	1.60	3¾	3.43	5¾	5.26	7¾	7.09	9¾	8.92
1⅞	1.71	3⅞	3.54	5⅞	5.37	7⅞	7.20	9⅞	9.03
2	1.83	4	3.66	6	5.49	8	7.32	10	9.14

INDEX